IRON RAILS, IRON MEN, AND THE RACE TO LINK THE NATION

IRON RAILS, IRON MEN,

AND THE

RACE TO LINK THE NATION

THE STORY OF THE TRANSCONTINENTAL RAILROAD

MARTIN W. SANDLER

CANDLEWICK PRESS

FOR CAROL

First edition 2015

Library of Congress Catalog Card Number 2014954533

ISBN 978-0-7636-6527-2

15 16 17 18 19 20 APS 10 9 8 7 6 5 4 3 2 1

Printed in Humen, Dongguan, China

This book was typeset in Century Old Style.

Candlewick Press
99 Dover Street
Somerville, Massachusetts 02144

visit us at www.candlewick.com

CONTENTS

PROLOGUE

The reporter could only stare in wonder at the scene before him. Here, on the vast American prairie, hundreds of workmen, with nothing but endless miles of grassland in front of them, were laying tracks. But it was not just the task; it was the way they were doing it, as he would later state, that filled him with "amusement, curiosity," and above all else, "profound respect."

"On they came," he wrote. "A light car, drawn by a single horse, gallops up to the front with its load of rails. Two men seize the end of a rail and start forward, the rest of the gang taking hold by twos, until it is clear of the car. They come forward at a run. At the word of command the rail is dropped in its place, right side up with care, while the same process goes on at the other side of the car. Less than thirty seconds to a rail, and so four rails go down [in a] minute. The moment the car is empty, it is tipped over on the side of the track to let the next loaded car pass it, and then it is tipped back again, and it is a sight to see it go flying back for another load, propelled by a horse at full gallop at the end of sixty or eighty feet of rope. Close behind the first gang come [the men who spike the rails to their wooden ties] and a lively time they make of it. It is a grand 'Anvil Chorus' that those sturdy sledges are playing across the plains. It is in triple time, three strokes to the spike . . . ten spikes to a rail, four hundred rails to a mile, eighteen hundred miles to San Francisco. Twenty-one million times are those sledges to be swung . . . before the great work of modern America is complete."

The reporter was right. The building of the transcon-

tinental railroad was not only America's greatest "work"; it was also one of the greatest and most daring adventures the nation had ever seen. It took place in an era when only trails and wagon tracks crossed more than two-thirds of the nation, a time when it took up to six months to cross the country. To build a railroad some 1,800 miles over the prairies, across the deserts, and through the mountains, if it could be done at all, would, as one of its advocates stated, require the work of "giants." There would indeed be "giants" involved, but the undertaking would be far more difficult than even these visionaries could have imagined. It would be made even more daunting by the greed, corruption, and violence that were also part of the experience. It would take more than six years, but in the end, the nation would be linked by two bands of steel. And things would never be the same.

Workers on the transcontinental railroad lay tracks across the American prairie. "These men," declared the New York Tribune, *"were working upon a scale never before approached in railway history."*

1

DREAMERS
AND
BUILDERS

No one knows for sure who the first person was to suggest a railroad that, by linking the East Coast with the West Coast, would "shrink the continent and change the whole world." It may have been Samuel Dexter, the editor of a small Michigan newspaper called the *Western Emigrant*. "It is in our power," Dexter wrote in 1832, "to open an immense interior country to market, to unite our Eastern and Western shores firmly together."

Another railroad enthusiast, Dr. Samuel Barlow, shared Dexter's vision. In an article published in a Westport, Massachusetts, weekly, he envisioned a railroad over which passengers could cross the entire three thousand miles of the United States in an unheard-of thirty days while traveling at the "incredible" speed of ten miles an hour. A transcontinental railroad, Barlow declared, would be "the greatest public work . . . that mortal man has ever yet accomplished."

Some ten years later, a wealthy New York businessman named Asa Whitney, a distant relative of Eli Whitney, who had invented the cotton gin, actually petitioned Congress for the building of such a railroad. Aside from linking the nation, Whitney saw another enormous benefit that a transcontinental railroad would bring. He had made much of his fortune by selling his products to China and bringing back such wanted goods as tea, spices, and silk. But he had been forced to endure the long months it took to exchange these products between East Coast ports and Asia by ship. A railroad to West Coast ports, he declared, would make the long and often dangerous ocean voyage to Asia much shorter and much more profitable. It would, in fact, open up the lucrative China trade to all American merchants.

Whitney did everything he could to convince Congress to authorize the railroad he envisioned. He even offered to build it at his own expense if he was given enough land in the West that he could then sell. Determined to prove that it could be done, he organized an expedition into the vast territory to explore the best possible route for his railroad to take.

It was all in vain. Even those few congressmen who believed that it just might be possible for such a railroad to be built could not agree on supporting Whitney. Southern congressmen insisted that it take a southern route. Others said that they could not even consider such a project unless the railroad passed through their city or state.

Whitney, Dexter, and Barlow were but three of at least a score of individuals who, in the 1830s and 1840s, made their feelings known about the enormous benefits a transcontinental railroad would bring to the nation. But understanding what such an iron road would do for the country was one thing; being able to build it was quite another.

The vast majority of government officials and almost all private citizens shared the same opinion: it simply couldn't be done. In response to a claim that a transcontinental railroad would "create settlements, commerce and wealth," the *Cincinnati Daily Gazette* declared that those making this claim might just as well be promising "to unite neighboring planets in our solar system and make them better acquainted with each other."

It was not difficult to understand why the newspaper's editors felt this way. The nation's existing railroad lines went no farther west than the Missouri River. The distance from that point to the Pacific was 1,800 miles. It wasn't just the staggering distance, though. Every railroad that had ever been built had been constructed to connect one city or town to another inhabited area. But between the Missouri River and the Pacific Ocean, except for significant Native American communities and Salt Lake City, there was not a single settlement of any real size. It was, as a Boston newspaper described it, "a big blank slate." A transcontinental railroad, if it could somehow be built, would be the first railroad ever constructed in advance of civilization.

And that was not all. Construction crews would have to lay tracks over some of the most difficult terrain on earth. Hundreds of miles of searing desert would have to be crossed. Even more challenging, as one early railroad historian wrote, "Any transcontinental railroad must cross two mountain chains popularly regarded as impossible barriers. Still fresh in the memory of emigrants who crawled westward were mountain trails so steep that wagons had to be lowered by rope. . . . Moreover, little was known of the principles of traction. Only a few years earlier, even engineers generally believed that gravity would defy any attempt to drive a locomotive uphill."

In order to build a railroad through these mountains, the highest bridges ever erected would have to be built. Tunnels through mountains of pure granite would have to be constructed. All this had to be accomplished without bulldozers, rock drills, or modern explosives. A transcontinental railroad would have to be built entirely by hand.

There were no trees on the hundreds of miles of the American prairie to use for railroad ties. There were no factories or foundries to manufacture rails anywhere near where the tracks would be laid. The millions of railroad ties, the miles and miles of iron rails, the enormously heavy steam locomotives, and almost everything else that would be required would have to be shipped to the building sites — from the east across the Missouri River, from the west all the way around Cape Horn in South America, a fifteen-thousand-mile voyage by sea.

And if this was not enough to discourage even the most ardent proponent of a railroad that would link the nation, there were other enormous challenges as well. Prominent among them was the weather that was certain to be encountered. On the plains, temperatures were known to rise to well over one hundred degrees Fahrenheit. Tornadoes destroyed everything in their path. In the mountains, temperatures dropped as low as thirty degrees below zero and snow piled up as high as sixty feet. And over miles and miles of the territory that would have to be crossed was the specter of what most struck fear into the hearts of all those who dared venture into the West — tens of thousands of Native Americans determined to keep

Weber Canyon, Utah. America's mountain ranges would present the greatest challenges in the creation of a transcontinental railroad.

intruders from encroaching upon land that was still their own. No wonder that when photographer and civil engineer John Plumbe sent his own proposal for a transcontinental railroad to Congress, one congressman stated that Plumbe's request was as far-fetched as asking the government "to build a railroad to the moon."

Well into the 1840s, the idea of a transcontinental railroad seemed an impossible one. Some of the nation's leading figures made a point of questioning the value of linking the heavily settled and "civilized" East with what they viewed as the sparsely settled, untamed West. Among them was

Massachusetts's legendary senator Daniel Webster. "What do we want with this region of savages and wild beasts, of deserts, of shifting sands and whirlwinds of dust, of cactus and prairie dogs," Webster asked his fellow senators. "To what use could we ever put these endless mountain ranges? . . . What could we do with the western coastline three thousand miles away, rockbound, cheerless and uninviting?"

Strong words, but in a nation still less than one hundred years old, things were changing rapidly. By 1850, California had developed to a point where it was admitted as a state. Oregon and other western territories stood poised to be admitted as well. Perhaps most important, gold had been discovered in California. "Gold fever" gripped the nation. Thousands of people from every part of the country, seeking to get rich, dropped whatever they were doing and headed for the goldfields. Some spent months walking all the way to California. Others went on horseback or in wagon trains. Those who could afford the high price of a ticket made the six-to-nine-month voyage by sailing vessel or steamship. Many others who had far less money boarded any type of vessel that would float. It was a phenomenon that lasted throughout the 1850s and one that the government could not help but notice. What if there had been a cross-country railroad over which these thousands of fortune seekers could have traveled? What if such a railroad had made it possible for the government itself to take advantage of the gold and particularly the other minerals that were being uncovered?

Suddenly the mood of the government changed. Reasons for building the railroad, including those first articulated by early visionaries like Asa Whitney, were revisited. They were perhaps expressed most clearly in a report commissioned by the California state senate. "A railroad, from some point on the Mississippi, or its tributaries, to some point on the bay of San Francisco," the report stated, "is the best route that can be adopted for the purpose of securing the Commerce of China or India. . . . It would also be the means of great daily intercourse between the East and West coast of this Republic. . . . It is the duty of this legislature to encourage the speedy building of a Railroad from the Atlantic to the Pacific, across the territory of the United States."

In 1856, a special committee of the Congress concluded that "the necessity that exists for constructing lines of railroad and telegraphic communication between the Atlantic and Pacific coasts of this continent is no longer a question for argument; it is conceded by every one." An 1853 article in the widely read *Putnam's Monthly Magazine* actually foresaw the committee's findings. "A railroad from the Mississippi to California or Oregon is a foregone conclusion," the article stated. "Stupendous as the enterprise seems, rivaling in grandeur and surpassing in usefulness any work that the genius of man has hitherto undertaken . . . it has been decided that it must be built. . . . Surveying parties, appointed by the Government to explore the routes are already on the ground." The surveyors had a most important assignment. The question of what route the railroad should take had become as vital an issue as whether the railroad should be built.

In March 1853, in an attempt to answer the question, the government instructed the secretary of war, Jefferson Davis, the man who seven years later would become president of the southern states in rebellion against the United States, to organize four separate surveying expeditions to determine which route would be the most "practicable and economical" to the Pacific. Each of the expeditions was a remarkable undertaking. Just one of them alone, led by army lieutenant Amiel Weeks Whipple, included seventy men, 250 mules, and a long train of large freight wagons. Whipple's scientific staff included not only surveyors but also geologists, botanists, astronomers, naturalists, and artists. As one journal would later report, "Not since Napoleon had taken his company of [scholars and experts] into Egypt had the world seen such an assemblage of scientists and technicians marshalled under one banner."

The surveying expeditions' findings were published in a twelve-volume set of books that contained detailed assessments of whether the land they had explored would provide a suitable path for a railroad. The books were also filled with many maps and artists' drawings and descriptions of wildlife, plants, and trees, as well as the Native American peoples they had encountered.

It was a marvelous achievement, providing the nation with the greatest amount of knowledge about the geography of the West it had ever received. But as far as the government was concerned, it was also a major disappointment. For in the end it was determined that none of the routes that had been explored was suitable for the building of the iron road. Ironically, the discovery of this vital route would come about not through the endeavors of hundreds of surveyors and scientists, but through the extraordinary efforts of two men, each very different from the other, operating half a continent apart.

Among those who had read the surveyors' reports with great interest was a twenty-eight-year-old civil engineer named Theodore Judah. With the help of one hundred workers, he had just supervised the construction of California's first railroad line in the foothills of the Sierra Nevada. When the twenty-one-mile-long line was completed, Judah had gone to the president of the new line and urged him to let him extend the line much farther. But, aware of the towering Sierra Nevada that lay ahead, the president turned him down. There was no way, he told Judah, that a railroad could be built through those mountains.

By 1853, when the route-seeking surveys had begun, Judah had joined the ranks of those who believed in the necessity of a transcontinental railroad. He had in fact become obsessed with the idea. He seemed to talk about it to anyone who would listen, so much so that, out of earshot, those around him began to refer to him as "Crazy Judah."

But Theodore Judah was not crazy. He was a visionary. And he was a realist as well. The United States needed a transcontinental railroad, and more than anything, he wanted to be a big part of its construction. He was well aware that of all the incredible challenges that building a railroad from coast to coast would present, the greatest would be laying tracks through the seemingly impenetrable Sierras. And he knew that a route through those mountains had to be found. The route would have to take into account drilling and blasting tunnels through solid-granite peaks, creating roadbeds around the peaks that were too long to be tunneled through, and constructing towering bridges over the Sierras' rivers and valleys.

Finding a route through the Sierras was a task that would have diminished the resolve of a less determined man. But Judah was convinced that such a route could be found. He began by hiking into the Sierras, spending days, even weeks living out in the open, enduring rain, wind, and, in the higher elevations, ice and driving snow. He mapped out a route, noting where tunnels, roadbeds, and bridges would need to be constructed.

At last he reached a point where he believed he could offer proof that a railroad through the Sierras could be built. But, as he well knew, finding a route was only the first step. Nothing could happen unless the enormous amount of money needed to finance the project could be raised.

THEODORE JUDAH

THEODORE DEHONE JUDAH and the American railroad came of age together. Born in Bridgeport, Connecticut, in 1826, a year before the Baltimore and Ohio, the nation's first railroad, came into being, Judah grew up in Troy, New York, where he displayed signs of genius at a remarkably early age. In 1837, when he was only eleven years old, he began taking advanced science classes at Rensselaer Polytechnic Institute. At the age of thirteen, he became a surveyor's assistant on the Schenectady and Troy Railroad. By the time he turned twenty-five, he had learned so much about what was increasingly being regarded as the marvel of the age that he was named chief engineer for the building of the Buffalo and New York Railroad. He completed that assignment so well that he was then asked to take on what many regarded as an impossible task—constructing a railroad beneath the famous Niagara Falls. Judah not only succeeded in surveying and directing the building of the Niagara Gorge Railroad; he also completed the job well ahead of schedule.

It did not take long for news of Judah's accomplishments to spread. He had in fact become one of the nation's most acclaimed railroad engineers. Among those most impressed with what he had achieved was the president of a company formed to construct California's first railroad, a twenty-one-mile line running from Sacramento to Folsom in the heart of the gold-mining country. In search of the best man to build the road, the president offered Judah the job.

Judah was thrilled. "Anna," he told his wife, "I am going to California to be the pioneer railroad engineer of the Pacific Coast." He would not only earn that distinction; he would, more than any other individual, become responsible for the birth of the transcontinental railroad.

Between 1856 and 1859, Judah made three trips to Washington hoping to persuade the government to supply the funds. To support his argument, he wrote and published, at his own expense, a pamphlet titled "A Practical Plan for Building the Pacific Railroad." He even set up a one-room Pacific Railroad Museum in the Capitol that included paintings of the areas over and through which his proposed railroad would travel, maps of preliminary routes he was considering, and geological specimens he had discovered. But by 1859, Congress had much more serious matters on its agenda. Despite the many different compromises that had been attempted, the northern and southern regions of the nation had grown further apart over the fact that slaveholders in the South refused to give up their slaves. Things had reached a boiling point, and the southern states were threatening to secede from the Union. After all his efforts, Judah's proposal fell on deaf ears.

He did not give up. If he couldn't get funding from the government, he would try to get it from private sources. In 1860, intent on producing an even more detailed map of his proposed route through the mountains, he went back into the Sierras. He not only created a highly detailed map that he felt would attract investors, but he also solved what he had previously considered to be the one troublesome problem in his mapping. He was not satisfied that he had found the best route for tracks to be laid through the treacherous Donner Pass. But here fortune smiled on him. In the midst of his new mapping, he received a letter from a druggist named Daniel Strong in which Strong offered to show him a way through the pass that would accommodate a railroad. Guiding Judah through the pass, Strong led the way to a ridge between two deep river valleys. A delighted Judah immediately realized that the ridge was wide enough for tracks to be laid upon it.

Convinced that he had mapped out a practical route through what he believed would be the most difficult terrain of all in constructing a transcontinental railroad, Judah drew up a document establishing a company to build a railroad. He named it the Central Pacific Railroad Company. He had a name but no money to back the company. In November of 1860, at a meeting of potential investors in a room above a Sacramento hardware store, four wealthy men agreed to put up the money necessary to get the Central Pacific Railroad Company started. Their names were Charles Crocker, Collis Huntington, Mark Hopkins, and Leland Stanford.

They were a diverse group of individuals. Crocker was an experienced and effective organizer of projects and men. Hopkins was an astute businessman. Stanford was a lawyer, who also had significant political influence. But it was Huntington who would eventually really run the Central Pacific while the transcontinental railroad was being built. It was he who would assume the critical role of seeing to it that supplies reached the Central Pacific work crews whenever and wherever they were needed. And it was he who would also continually lobby Congress for more financial support for the Central Pacific.

Although Judah had his initial funding, he still needed the government's support. Again he headed for Washington, hoping to at last convince the government to give him the bulk of the money his new company still needed. This time he got a very different reception because the nation's political situation had changed dramatically. The South had indeed seceded from the Union; the Civil War had begun. No longer were there Southern congressmen in Washington committed to blocking any cross-country railroad that took a northern route.

Most important, the new American president, Abraham Lincoln, was a strong champion of a transcontinental railroad. Though many in Congress were opposed to undertaking such a costly and difficult project in the midst of a civil war, Lincoln believed that, just as the war was being fought to unite the North and the South, an iron road across the country would bind East and West. It would make Americans across the nation feel like one people. "A railroad to the Pacific Ocean," he stated, "is imperatively demanded in the interests of the whole country. . . . The Federal Government ought to render immediate and efficient aid in its construction."

On July 1, 1862, Lincoln put that "immediate and efficient aid" into law when he signed the Pacific Railway Act. It authorized the Central Pacific Railroad to lay tracks from Sacramento to 150 miles beyond the California-Nevada border. And it created a whole new company to be called the Union Pacific Railroad Company. It would lay its rails westward until the two companies joined tracks. The government would pay each company $16,000 for each mile of track it laid in flat territory and $32,000 for each mile of track laid in the mountains. In addition, for each forty-mile section of track it completed, each company would be given thousands of acres of government-owned land that it could sell to people who wanted to settle on it. With one stroke of his pen, Abraham Lincoln had made the construction of a transcontinental railroad a reality.

President Lincoln had done something else as well. By authorizing the Central Pacific to begin laying its tracks eastward and creating the Union Pacific to set down rails westward, he had set the stage for an extraordinary race to see which company would lay the most miles of track before the two sides of the country were linked. It would become the most dramatic and most heralded race the nation had ever known.

THE BIG FOUR

As the Pacific Railway Act became law, the United States Congress issued a proclamation publicly thanking Theodore Judah for having made the act possible. But gratified as he was, Judah knew that the real work was just beginning. Informing his new partners that the railroad bill had been passed, he said, "We have drawn the elephant, now let us see if we can harness him up."

With Stanford as president, Huntington as vice president, Hopkins as treasurer, and Crocker as construction supervisor, the Central Pacific's Big Four appeared to be the perfect team to make the vision of a transcontinental railroad a reality. As Huntington would later write, "Each [of us] complemented each other in something the other lacked. There was Stanford, for instance, a man . . . who loved to deal with people. He was a good lawyer. There was Mark Hopkins. He was a thrifty man. Then, there was Crocker, the organizer, the executive, the director of men." Huntington himself, who would become the real boss of the company, possessed a world of business knowledge.

Pictured from left to right: Leland Stanford, Collis Huntington, Mark Hopkins, and Charles Crocker

As much as the Big Four believed that the nation should have a cross-country railroad, they also wanted to make as much money out of the project as they possibly could. And they were willing to use any means, no matter how devious, to enrich themselves. To his dismay, Judah realized that it had been easier to chart his way through the mountains than it would be to overcome the unbridled greed of the men with whom he had allied himself.

From the beginning, the Big Four held meetings without Judah's knowledge. They didn't want him to know about the dishonest things they were planning to do. Soon after Leland Stanford became president of the Central Pacific, he was elected governor of California. Almost immediately he used the power of his office to illegally transfer more than a million dollars of state funds into the Central Pacific's treasury. And Collis Huntington, knowing that the Central Pacific would be paid according to the number of miles of track it laid, began to make plans to bribe geologists to grossly overstate how many miles of rail the company set down.

By the fall of 1863, Judah had had enough. Appalled by his colleagues' behavior, he left for San Francisco and sailed to New York, where he hoped to find new investors who would buy the Big Four out. If the railroad that Judah had set in motion had been in place, his trip would have been a relatively quick and easy one. But in the fall of 1863, his best option was to sail to Panama, take a train to the Atlantic coast of that isthmus, and then travel by ship to New York.

Tragically, while crossing Panama, Judah contracted the dreaded yellow fever. He became so ill that when he arrived in New York, he was taken on a stretcher directly to his hotel. It was while he was lying there that the first rails of the Central Pacific line were laid. But Judah never heard about it. The man who had made it all possible died before the news could reach him.

Charlie Crocker, the construction supervisor, would be on the scene for the entire building of the great iron road. He took to his new job with a passion. He had never worked in construction, but he had spent several years in the California mining fields, where he had earned a reputation for toughness and for taking on any task, no matter how difficult. "I had all the experience necessary," Crocker would later state. "I knew how to manage men; I had worked them in the ore beds, in the coal pits, and worked them all sorts of ways, and had worked myself right along with them." At his side was construction boss James Strobridge, who was equally demanding of the labor force.

James Strobridge and Charles Crocker had an enormous problem. The Central Pacific's board of directors had failed to supply them with a large enough labor force. Crocker had managed to hire a number of unemployed Irishmen, but there were only five hundred of them, and every week more and more of them suddenly left to seek their fortunes in the Nevada silver mines. A desperate Crocker tried to solve the problem by placing an advertisement in the California newspapers. "Wanted," it read. "5,000 laborers for constant and permanent work, also experienced foremen. Apply to J. H. Strobridge, Superintendent. On the work, near Auburn."

He got only a few hundred responses. Most able-bodied men were off in the mountains, hoping to strike it rich in the silver mines. More desperate than ever, Crocker came up with an idea. There were more than fifty-five thousand Chinese people living in California. Tens of thousands had been lured there by the gold strikes in the late 1840s and early 1850s. When the gold ran out, many had taken jobs as laborers, gardeners, domestic workers, and fishermen. Because the Chinese population referred to their homeland as the "Celestial Kingdom," Californians called them Celestials. And because of differences in the way they looked, spoke, and conducted themselves, most of them had been victims of racial prejudice and discrimination. But not even their detractors could deny that Chinese men had a great capacity for work.

Crocker wanted to hire them for the Central Pacific, but he ran into stiff opposition from Strobridge, who believed that most Chinese men were too small and too fragile to tackle such heavy and exhausting work. Besides, stated Strobridge, they knew nothing about building a railroad. "I will not boss Chinese," Strobridge declared.

Crocker had a ready answer. "They built the Great Wall of China, didn't they?" he responded. "And people who could do that ought to be able to build a railroad." Finally, the two men reached a compromise. They would hire fifty Chinese laborers on a trial basis and see how they worked out.

JAMES STROBRIDGE

JAMES STROBRIDGE, the man Charles Crocker chose to be the Central Pacific's construction boss, was a burly Irishman from Vermont. At the age of sixteen, he began working as a tracklayer on the Vermont Central Railway and then helped build other railroad lines in New England. When gold was discovered in California in 1849, Strobridge, like thousands of others, raced to the goldfields. Failing to strike it rich, he tried his hand at farming, freighting, and canal building before becoming a construction foreman on the San Francisco and San Jose Railroad.

Strobridge, called Stro by his friends, was a rough-and-ready man who often carried a pick handle with him to settle disputes. Fond of saying that "men generally earn their money when they work for me," he was a most demanding boss. But he would prove to be the perfect man to guide and prod a unique army of laborers through some of the most difficult tasks any construction workers had ever been asked to perform.

Strobridge would have the distinction of being the only man from either the Central Pacific or the Union Pacific to have a home life throughout the entire building of the road. His wife, Hanna Maria Strobridge, and their six children traveled with him in a boxcar pulled by a locomotive. The Strobridges had converted the car into a three-bedroom house on wheels. Mrs. Strobridge had then refined it by adding a front porch complete with an awning, hanging plants, and a caged canary swinging from the rafters.

James Strobridge checks the progress of one of his work crews from a lofty perch. "The truth is," Charles Crocker would say, "there can't be a thing done unless it suits Strobridge."

The San Francisco newspaper the *Alta California* described the living quarters as a house that "would not discredit San Francisco."

The homey presence of Strobridge's family did not have the effect of moderating his foul language or fierce temper. Nor did it stop him from working twelve to fourteen hours a day as the boss of what would become the largest single workforce in America. And Hanna Strobridge earned her own distinction. Referred to by the workers as "the heroine of the CP," she became the only woman to travel the route of either line during its construction.

Hanna Strobridge (second from the left) stands on the porch-like platform running along the side of the railroad car that she converted into a home on the tracks.

When the first Chinese men arrived, Strobridge, convinced that they were too frail to swing heavy sledgehammers or pickaxes, put them to work doing simple tasks such as filling dump carts. Surprised at how quickly they carried out their tasks without a hint of complaint, Strobridge decided to test them further by having them attempt to prepare a roadbed on which tracks could be laid. The result was even more surprising to him. The roadbed the Chinese workers laid down was longer and much smoother than the ones the Irish workers had been able to construct. Then Strobridge decided to put the Chinese to the ultimate test by having them blast rock. Not only did they handle this dangerous assignment without a hitch; they actually seemed to enjoy it. Reporting on what he had seen these initial Chinese laborers accomplish, one of Crocker's engineers stated simply, "The experiment has proved eminently successful."

Convinced that they had found the solution to their serious labor problem, Strobridge and Crocker sent agents throughout the Pacific coast seeking to find as many Chinese workers as they could. They also contacted agents who specialized in finding laborers overseas and commissioned them to obtain Chinese workers for the Central Pacific. It would be a time-consuming process and it would not be until January 1865 that Chinese laborers would join the CP's ranks in great numbers, but eventually more than ten thousand Chinese men would make up almost 90 percent of the Central Pacific's workforce.

Hiring the Chinese workers turned out to be the most important decision the Central Pacific made in meeting the challenges of building the transcontinental railroad. The Chinese men were not only magnificent workers; they were also more dependable and more willing to take on any task, no matter how difficult or dangerous, than almost any of the others who labored on the great road. And there was something else, something that was also extremely important. Throughout the almost seven years of the transcontinental's construction, the Chinese men would remain far healthier than most of the other workers. It was probably because of their diet and habits. The food that the Irish workers ate was supplied to them by the Central Pacific. It consisted mostly of beef, beans, and potatoes. There were no fresh vegetables. It was hardly a healthy diet. The Irishmen quenched the constant thirst that arose from their heavy labors by drinking from the streams and lakes they encoun-

Chinese workers transport cartloads of dirt as they conduct grading operations in an area of the Sierra Nevada known as Prospect Hill.

tered. The water was often brackish and full of harmful bacteria. Many of the Irish workers would lose time on the job as a result of the dysentery they got from drinking the tainted water.

The Chinese diet was altogether different. Even though, because of the prejudicial feelings of the times, the Chinese were paid less than the Irish, each of their work crews hired its own cook. One of his duties was to purchase a wide variety of healthy foods from the Chinese districts in San Francisco and Sacramento. The workers' diet included fish, bean sprouts, mushrooms, rice, and cabbage. The cooks even kept pigs and chickens so that on weekends fresh pork, bacon, and poultry could be served.

Equally important, the Chinese laborers never drank water directly from the streams and lakes. Instead, they drank hot tea. It was a good drink of choice because boiling the water for it removed bacteria and other harmful elements. The tea was carried to the work sites in huge barrels suspended from each end of a bamboo pole balanced on the shoulders of special members of the crews called tea boys.

Thanks to the Chinese workforce, the labor problem that had so plagued the Central Pacific had been solved, and in a way that neither Strobridge nor Crocker nor the other directors of the CP could have ever hoped for. Among those who recognized what the Chinese workers meant to the CP was the company's president, Leland Stanford. For years he had bitterly opposed Chinese immigration. Now he publicly proclaimed that it would be of great benefit if at least half a million Chinese were allowed to immediately enter the country.

On January 8, 1863, still long before Chinese workers began joining the CP's ranks, the Central Pacific officially began laying tracks. Thousands of Californians traveled to Sacramento to look on as Leland Stanford ceremoniously shoveled the first load of dirt, signifying the beginning of the laying of a roadbed (called grading) for the first section of tracks. On October 26, 1863, another milestone took place when Strobridge's men spiked the CP's first rails to their ties. But this time there was no ceremony. Even this early on, it had become all too clear that being able to lay tracks over and through the mountains was far from a certainty. The decision to omit a ceremony was made by Collis Huntington. "If you want to jubilate in driving the first spike, go ahead and do it. I don't," he had telegraphed Crocker. "These mountains look too ugly and I see too much work ahead. We may fail and I want to have as few people know it as we can and if we get up a jubilation any little nobody can drive the first spike, but there are many months of hard labor and unrest between the first and the last spike."

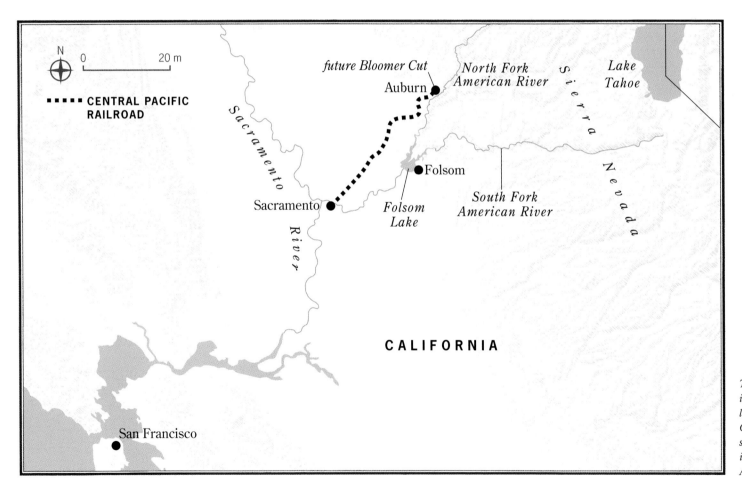

The Central Pacific began its long, difficult track-laying in Sacramento, California, after having set up its base camp for its construction crews in Auburn.

2

RAILS ACROSS THE PLAINS

Before Theodore Judah died, he had pointed out the way that tracks could begin to be laid from west to east across the United States. But what about a route from east to west? Long before there was a Pacific Railway Act, Grenville Dodge had made discoveries that would lead to the establishment of that route. He would play an even greater role than Judah in making the transcontinental railroad a reality.

Dodge was a great supporter of the notion of a railroad that linked the nation. In 1853, while on a surveying mission for a budding railway, he made the first of many discoveries that convinced him that a transcontinental railroad was possible. He had just completed his survey when, standing near what is today Independence, Missouri, he made an abrupt decision. Intrigued by the wilderness he had just encountered, he decided to keep moving westward to see where he would end up. After several days, alone on horseback, he stopped at the top of a high cliff. The sight beneath him took his breath away. Spread out below was the Missouri River, twisting

The Union Pacific broke ground for its tracks westward on December 2, 1863. However, it would be eighteen months before the UP would begin laying tracks through the Platte River Valley and across the Great Plains.

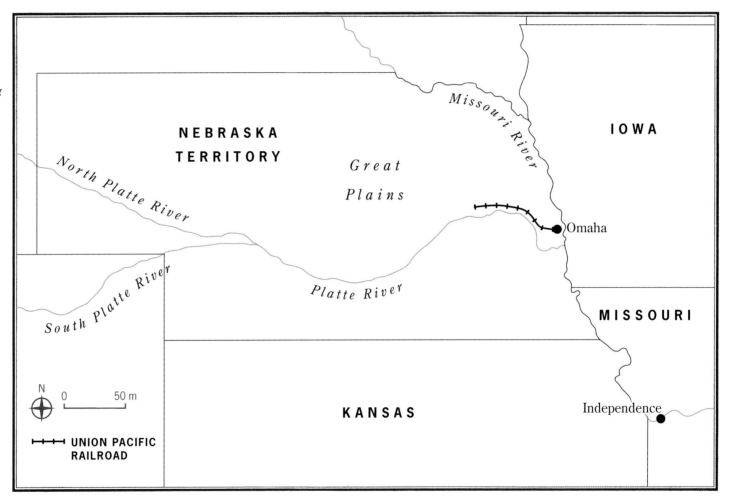

NEBRASKA
TERRITORY

Missouri River

IOWA

*Great
Plains*

North Platte River

Omaha

South Platte River

Platte River

MISSOURI

N
0   50 m

KANSAS

Independence

⊢+++⊣ UNION PACIFIC
RAILROAD

and turning into the distance. Beyond, to the west, as far as his eyes could see, lay the Platte River Valley and the enormous, empty plains. He realized, as he later wrote, that this was the site of the route first "made by buffalo, next used by the Indians, then by the fur traders, next by the Mormons, and then by the overland immigration to California and Oregon." This, he thought, would be the perfect place for a cross-country railroad to begin its march westward across the plains, past the Rocky Mountains, and into the Utah and Oregon territories. The biggest challenge, he knew, would be getting tracks through the formidable Rockies.

In 1866, Dodge would solve that problem as well. Now a post–Civil War general in the United States army, Dodge was leading a small party on a scouting mission through a section of the Rockies through which few white men had ever passed, when he had a most unexpected experience. "I took a few mounted men—I think six," Dodge later wrote, "and with one of my scouts as guide, went up . . . to the summit of Cheyenne Pass, striking south along the crest of the mountains to obtain a good view of the country. . . . About noon, in the valley of a tributary of Crow Creek, we discovered Indians, who, at the same time, discovered us. . . . We dismounted and started down the ridge, holding the Indians at bay, when they came too near, with our [rifles] . . . [We] followed this ridge out until I discovered it led down to the plains without a break. I then said to my guide that if we saved our scalps I believed we had found [a way through these mountains]."

He was right. Just as Theodore Judah, with the help of Daniel Strong, had solved one of the thorniest problems in finding a route through the Sierras, Grenville Dodge had come upon an avenue through the Rockies upon which, difficult as it would be, a railroad could be built.

GRENVILLE DODGE

GRENVILLE MELLEN DODGE was born near Danvers, Massachusetts, in 1831. He was only fourteen when he helped explorer Frederick Lander survey a railway line. Impressed with his young assistant's abilities, Lander encouraged Dodge to enter Norwich University to study engineering. He graduated from Norwich in 1851 and moved to Council Bluffs, Iowa, to conduct surveys for several railroads. His explorations soon caught the attention of Abraham Lincoln. In August 1859, Dodge was in Pine Bluffs, Iowa, when he met presidential candidate Lincoln. "Mr. Lincoln," Dodge would later write, "sat down beside me and, by his kindly ways, soon drew from me all that I knew of the country west, and the results of my reconnaissances."

Dodge joined the Union army as a colonel in the Fourth Iowa Volunteer Infantry Regiment and eventually rose to the rank of major general. It was his contributions as a builder and repairer of military railroads that earned him the greatest distinction. Dodge took to the task with such dedication that at one point his crews repaired more than one hundred miles of track and 182 bridges in forty days. Throughout the war, when someone asked where Dodge was, the common reply became "We don't know where he is, but we can tell where he has been."

In 1866, while fully occupied with his UP duties, Dodge was elected to the United States Congress. He had never campaigned for that office and, totally engrossed in seeing the transcontinental through to completion, never really served in the post.

By the time Dodge had made this discovery, many of his accomplishments, particularly his genius at railroad building, had become known. Among Dodge's greatest admirers was a man named Thomas Durant. The two had met several times when Dodge was carrying out his prewar surveying. Neither man, however, could have had any idea of how closely the future would bring them together.

When, through the Pacific Railway Act of 1862, Congress had established the Union Pacific Railroad, it had stipulated that it was to be run by a board of directors. And just as the Big Four controlled the Central Pacific, one member of that board would come to control the Union Pacific. That man was Thomas Durant.

Congress had left it up to President Lincoln to select the place where the UP would begin laying its rails. On November 17, 1863, Lincoln picked Omaha, Nebraska. On December 2, 1863, Durant turned over the Union Pacific's first shovelful of earth. A huge crowd roared its approval, soldiers fired enthusiastic salutes, and one speaker proclaimed that the transcontinental railroad was the "greatest enterprise under God." It was a gala beginning, but it would be a full year and a half before the Union Pacific would begin laying down its tracks.

The frustratingly long delay was caused by several factors. High on the list was the fact that the UP was having a serious problem finding the right men to lead the railroad's construction. Throughout the Civil War, Durant had been attempting to lure his friend Dodge away from the army. Finally, in early 1866, he succeeded, and Dodge joined the Union Pacific as its chief engineer. What he discovered was a company that, just like the Central Pacific at its start, was having great difficulty assembling the thousands of workers needed for the enormous task ahead.

THOMAS DURANT

THOMAS CLARK DURANT was both a brilliant organizer and a scoundrel. Born in Lee, Massachusetts, in 1820, he graduated from Albany Medical College but he had no intention of spending a lifetime in medicine. His great ambition was to make money. After a short stint in a medical office, he became a director of Durant, Lathrop and Company, a grain-exporting company based in New York. But he saw his real opportunity to make his fortune by gaining control of the Union Pacific.

When the UP was formed in 1862, Major General John Dix was named the company's president. But Dix was far too occupied as commander of the Union forces to pay sufficient attention to the company. As the UP's vice president and general manager, Durant became the real head of the Union Pacific.

One of the provisions of the Pacific Railway Act of 1862 was that no person could own more than $200,000 worth of stock in the company. Acting in the same illicit manner as the CP's Big Four, Durant lent money to his friends, persuaded them to buy UP stock, and then had them secretly sell the stock back to him. This way he became UP's largest stockholder.

Durant and some fellow stockholders set up a construction company called the Crédit Mobilier. Through this company, they secretly awarded themselves the contract to build the UP's portion of the transcontinental. Each time the government paid for miles of track laid, a portion of the money was funneled to Durant and others to whom he had either sold or given stock. To ensure that there would be no government investigation, Durant gave significant amounts of stock in the Crédit Mobilier to key politicians and government officials. Included among them were the future vice president of the United States Schuyler Colfax; several members of Congress; and the future president of the United States James Garfield.

As soon as he assumed his duties, Dodge set about solving the labor shortage by tapping into a huge source that had become available. A devastating potato famine had forced thousands of Irishmen to flee their country and seek new opportunities in America. Once across the Atlantic, they had begun filling up the cities along the eastern seaboard. Anxious for work, Irish laborers by the thousands joined the Union Pacific work crews. It would be a most fortunate development. Just as the Chinese workers would prove themselves so successful in tackling the mountains, the Irish laborers would meet the challenges of building a railroad across the plains. As poet Stephen Vincent Benét would observe: "They were strong men [who] built the Big Road [across the plains] . . . and it was the Irish [that] did it. [They] could swing a pick all day and dance all night, if there was a fiddler handy. . . . [They] liked the strength and wildness of it—would drink with the thirstiest and fight with the wildest. . . . It was all meat and drink to [them]."

And with the Civil War at last over, Dodge was able to turn to another labor source. In 1866, legions of veterans of the conflict found themselves abruptly out of work. Thousands were unmarried men with no obligations back home. Before the war, many had never left home and, despite the horrific aspects of the war, they had gotten caught up in the adventure of it all. Now they were seeking new excitement. And what bolder and riskier undertaking could there be than building a railroad across an unimaginable wilderness?

The men who were called upon to construct an iron road across so many miles into the unknown had to be willing to accept discipline, take orders, and operate with military precision. After long years of war, the Civil War veterans had, of necessity, acquired all these abilities.

Workers pose in front of the Union Pacific's paymaster's car. While their wages were, of course, important to them, many of the Union Pacific's laborers had signed on for the sheer adventure of building the great iron road.

As Grenville Dodge would later write, "The organization for the Union Pacific Railroad was upon a military basis, [so many men] upon it had been in the Civil War; the heads of most of the engineering parties and all chiefs of the construction forces were officers in the Civil War; the chief of the track laying force . . . had been a distinguished division commander in the Civil War, and at any moment I could call into the field a thousand men, well officered, ready to meet any crisis or any emergency."

The UP was organized like an army. What was needed was a man who could lead it. Fortunately, Durant and Dodge had found such a man. His name was Jack Casement.

JACK CASEMENT

OF ALL THE TENS OF THOUSANDS of men who built the transcontinental railroad, John Stephen "Jack" Casement was the most colorful character. Tough as nails, Casement dressed like a Russian Cossack. He carried a bullwhip and always wore a revolver in his belt. Even though he was only five feet four inches tall, he stood ten feet tall as a leader of men.

Casement was born in Geneva, New York, in 1829. When he was seventeen, he began working on a railroad as a tracklayer, and at nineteen, he was promoted to construction foreman.

Casement was extremely close to his younger brother Dan, who also became a railroad worker. By the late 1850s, the Casement brothers were responsible for overseeing the construction of the Sunbury and Erie Railroad and the Erie and Pittsburgh Railroad. They gained national attention when one of their construction gangs laid three miles of track in a single day.

Jack Casement entered the Union army as a major in the Seventh Ohio Infantry. During the conflict he led more than four hundred men out of an enemy trap, earning a promotion to brigadier general. His ability to organize both men and large undertakings served him well as the construction boss of the Union Pacific.

Jack Casement, whip in hand, stands beside his construction train. Note the photographer's wagon at the right.

One of Casement's first accomplishments was to create a special train that would travel the entire construction route. Called the perpetual train, it was the heart, and the brain, of the entire operation.

No one had ever seen anything like Casement's creation. Pushed, rather than pulled, by a huge locomotive, it had more than twenty cars. At the front of the train, closest to the tracklaying, were flatcars that carried scores of different tools and other equipment. The blacksmith's shop was also perched on one of these cars.

Next came the strangest cars of all, the three rolling bunkhouses where many of the workers lived. Specially built in the Union Pacific's shops in Omaha, they were each eighty-five feet long, ten feet wide, and eight feet from floor to ceiling. Each was lined with triple tiers of bunks in which the workmen slept. The three cars had no windows, and on hot nights they became stifling. On these evenings, many of their inhabitants took to erecting makeshift tents on the train's roofs so they could sleep in the open air. Others slung hammocks under the train. It was also not uncommon for many of the men to escape their sweltering quarters by pitching tents beside the tracks.

Following the bunkhouses came the dining car. Its special feature was a long single table that ran the full length of the car. Here the men ate in shifts, 125 at a time. They had to eat quickly in order to make room for the next group so that everyone got back on the job on time. As a reporter for the *New-York Evening Post* noted, it made for a lively scene, especially at breakfast, when the men had to first be awakened. "It is half past five and time for the hands to be waked up," the reporter wrote. "This is done by ringing a bell on the sleeping car until everyone turns out and by giving the fellows under the car a smart kick and by pelting the fellows in the tents on the top with bits of clay. In a very few minutes they are all out stretching and yawning. Another bell and they crowd in for breakfast. The table is lighted by hanging lamps, for it is yet hardly daylight. At intervals of about a yard are wooden buckets of coffee, great plates of bread and platters of meat. There is no ceremony: every man dips his cup into the buckets of coffee and sticks his own fork into whatever is nearest him. If a man has got enough and is through, he quietly puts one foot on the middle of the table and steps across."

The dining car had another feature, one that was also part of each of the bunkhouses. In every handy spot there were long racks holding rifles. Between them, the bunkhouses and the dining car held more than a thousand of these weapons, ready to be used in the event of an attack by Native Americans. The cars in the rest of the train housed kitchens, pantries, storerooms, engineers' offices, and carpenters' shops. One car served as Casement's working quarters.

As the train made its way across the plains, it was trailed by horse-drawn wagons carrying additional provisions and supplies. Bringing up the rear was a herd of some five hundred cattle that would provide the crews their hefty meals.

The creation of the construction train was a positive step in preparing the UP's crews for the enormous task that lay ahead of them. But even the most optimistic of the workers and their bosses knew that there would be extraordinary challenges. High on the list would be keeping the construction crews fully supplied with the tons of materials they needed to carry out their work. They would be crossing the plains for more than fifteen hundred miles, and with each passing mile, they would be moving farther away from the sources of their vital supplies. "To supply one mile

There were other serious challenges as well. Weather was certainly one of them. In winter, the plains could be as bitterly cold and as blizzard prone as the high mountains in which the Central Pacific was now struggling. In the summer, temperatures could reach over one hundred degrees Fahrenheit and remain there for days, sometimes weeks.

And then there were the insects. As any of those in Casement's army who had spent time on the prairie knew all too well, the plains were swarming with the creatures. Among them were huge horseflies that tormented the workmen and drove their horses and mules to distraction. Worse yet were the billions of grasshoppers that periodically swept across the plains. On more than one occasion, they covered the tracks in such enormous numbers that even the heaviest locomotives would skid out of control.

Of all the challenges the railroad crews faced, the one that put fear in the hearts of even the bravest workers was the threat of attack by native people who lived along the railroad's route. The plains were home to millions of Native Americans—Sioux, Comanche, Arapaho, Pawnee, Paiute, Cheyenne, Kiowa, and other nations. Mounted on horseback, these Plains Indians were regarded by American army officers as the best light cavalry in the world. For generations they had resisted white encroachment into their lands. Now the appearance of thousands of railroad workers and the portent of what the tracks they were laying would mean represented the greatest intrusion they had ever faced.

The coming of the railroad would leave the world of the West forever changed. It would bring more and more European-American settlers to the plains, resulting in forced removals, bloodshed, legal battles, and, ultimately, the destruction of the Plains Indians' way of life.

A linchpin of this destruction, and symbol of it, was the fate of the

North American buffalo. As late as the mid-1800s, tens of millions of buffalo roamed the American plains. They were so numerous that just one herd could stretch for twenty-five miles. The buffalo were at the heart of the Plains Indians' existence. They had built their cultures, communities, and way of life around the animals and depended on the many products they derived from them for food, clothing, tools, and shelter.

The presence of the buffalo, however, posed a problem for the transcontinental railroad workers. The huge animals not only blocked the path of the rails; they also seriously damaged the tracks once they'd been laid. Killing off as many buffalo as possible became a high priority among those intent on driving the rails across the plains.

And the millions of settlers who would follow in the railroad's wake would only deepen the threat to the buffalo. The settlers would come to the plains to farm. They weren't interested in the buffalo except as an animal to be hunted for sport, and they had no objections to the eventual slaughter of the buffalo by hunters and sportsmen to the brink of extinction.

The decimation of the buffalo herds was a tragedy to the Plains Indians. At a meeting with government officials, a Crow chief named Bear's Tooth spoke for his fellow leaders when he implored: *"Achan! Achan! Achan!* Father! Father! Father! Listen well. Your young men have gone on the path and have . . . killed my game and my buffalo. They did not kill them to eat; they left them to rot where they fell. Father, were I to go to your country to kill your cattle, what would you say? . . . Father, you talk about farming, I don't want to hear it; I was raised on buffalo and I love it. Since I was born I was raised like your chiefs, to be strong, to move my camps when necessary, to roam over the prairie at will. Take pity upon us; I am tired of talking."

Bear Tooth's words fell on deaf ears. The buffalo would be massacred as never before. With each mile of track laid, the Indians' ages-old ability to "roam over the prairie at will" would be dramatically diminished.

But across the plains the UP's army of workers marched. First came the surveyors, engineers, axmen, flagmen, and hunters, working hundreds of miles ahead of the rest. They blazed the way through terribly difficult, often dangerous country few white men had ever seen. Their job was to set the exact line where the graders could carve out their roadbeds and the tracklayers could set down their rails.

Being at the vanguard of the construction army provided the adventure that many of the surveyors and those who accompanied them sought. They encountered acres of grass that grew more than ten feet high. They came upon prairie-dog villages that stretched for more than ten miles. They came face-to-face with rock formations the shapes of which defied description. But every mile they traveled carried the potential for danger. In the warm weather, a prairie fire, moving across the grass-filled plains with the speed of a locomotive, could erupt at any time, threatening anything in its path. One young surveyor called them "a grand and appalling sight." In the winter months, the surveying crews were confronted with a different kind of danger. Temperatures on the plains dropped so low that, on more than one occasion, surveyors had their fingers freeze tight onto their measuring instruments. In one of the most bizarre incidents of all, an entire surveying party had to flee for their lives when a herd of some two thousand wild cattle suddenly appeared and stampeded through their tents. In one of his diary entries, young surveyor Arthur Ferguson noted that six of the surveying party had drowned, one had died as the result of a fall, and forty-five had been killed by American Indians.

Grenville Dodge stated that his surveyors "not only perform [their] duty well, but intelligently." Carrying out these duties in difficult terrain also required enormous physical strength.

Through it all, the surveyors and those who assisted them operated with one constant thought: everything depended on them. The army of workers that followed would not be able to carry out its various tasks unless the surveyors did their job. Far behind the surveyors, but still as many as three miles ahead of the tracklayers, came the graders. Their job was to construct the roadbed upon which the tracks would be laid. It was one of the most demanding of all the construction tasks, particularly when carried out on the open plains under the blistering sun. Working with pickaxes, shovels, scrapers, wheelbarrows, dump carts, horses, and mules, the graders dug away all obstacles that stood in the way of their building the smoothest surface possible for the rails. Each roadbed they created had to be more than two feet above the ground so that it would not flood in storms. All this required digging tons of dirt by hand, removing it from the site of the roadbed, and dumping it. The sight of hundreds of wheelbarrow-toting graders lined up waiting for their "barrows" to be filled with dirt was one of the greatest spectacles of the entire construction.

Because the final grade had to be unerringly level, all the work of the grading crews was carried out under the watchful eyes of various types of grading bosses. The dumping boss, who had to have the best eyesight of all, pointed with his shovel to the exact spot where he wanted wheelbarrows full of dirt dumped. He then used his shovel to level off each mound of dirt.

The supervisors, who constantly checked on the graders, were called walking bosses. They were specially selected for their ability to prod the men into working as hard and as quickly as they could. They were joined by the stable bosses, who were in charge of the hundreds of horses and mules and of the men who drove the wagons that the animals pulled back

The photographer titled this picture "Graders' Cabins." Graders most commonly worked far ahead of the tracklaying crews that followed them.

and forth to the grading sites with equipment and supplies. Overseeing all the graders and their bosses was the man known as the boarding boss. He was held accountable for the entire grading operation.

Well behind the grading crews came scores of sturdy horse-drawn wagons. Each of them was piled high with the heavy railroad ties that would be placed on top of the grade and upon which the tracks would be set in place. Once the ties were set down, wheeled flatcars, pulled by horses and often driven by the youngest members of Casement's army,

Historian Maury Klein wrote of the different groups of workers in Casement's army, "What unites them all is a fierce determination not to let down those coming on behind." Here, Union Pacific graders work to complete their difficult task, knowing that the tracklayers will not be far behind.

drew up to where the ties had been placed. They were filled with rails and spikes. Each of the flatcars had rollers on their sides to facilitate the unloading of the heavy iron rails. The burly tracklayers would take up their positions, five to each rail on each side of the track.

At the command "Down," the tracklayers would lift a five-hundred-to-seven-hundred-pound rail onto each side of the ties. It was a task that required enormous strength. Yet so expert were the tracklayers at carrying out the job, that more often than not, they dropped the rails in almost perfect position. It was a sight that never failed to capture the attention of the newsmen who were on the scene. "[The crew chief] calls out 'Down,' in a tone that equals the 'Forward' to an army," a reporter for the *Cincinnati Gazette* wrote. "Every thirty seconds there came that brave 'Down,' 'Down,' on either side of the track. They were the pendulum beats of a mighty era; they marked the time of the march and its regulation beat."

No sooner had each set of rails been set down than the gaugers stepped forward. Armed with their notched wooden gauges, they made certain that the rails were perfectly aligned to fit the locomotive wheels that would soon be racing upon them. Right behind them came the spikers, who used sledgehammers to pound long spikes through the rails and ties into the ground: three strokes to a spike, ten spikes to a rail, four hundred rails to a mile.

Gazing on Casement's army as it began to make its march across the plains, Grenville Dodge shook his head in wonder. "It was," he exclaimed, "the best organized, best equipped and best disciplined work force I have ever seen."

Each task carried out by the construction army was essential to the success of the entire undertaking, but the most admired workers of all were the tracklayers. As Charles Crocker stated, "Nothing looks to the public as much like making a railroad as the work of laying down iron on the roadbed."

3

ATTACKING THE MOUNTAINS

Half a continent away, the Central Pacific's workers were attempting to make their own march forward. It did not take them long to begin to realize how difficult their task would be or to demonstrate how willing they were to meet it. "We put up a high . . . bridge, 100 feet in height," CP construction worker A. P. Partridge later recounted. "With a heavy storm and a big fall of rain there was a lake on the hill above the bridge and when it filled it broke loose. Down everything came and swept away . . . the center of our bridge. That bridge had to be replaced. . . . Well, we went to the woods and hewed the timber . . . then got some ox teams and hauled it to the bridge and repaired the break."

CP crews had managed to set down only thirty-four miles of rails when, at the beginning of April 1864, they came face-to-face with an eight-hundred-foot-long, sixty-three-foot-deep mass of solid rock. In order to blast the way for laying tracks through what they named Bloomer Cut, the Chinese and Irish laborers had to use as much as five hundred kegs of black blasting powder a day. The rock and debris from each blast had to be removed by hand, one wheelbarrow at a time. It was at Bloomer Cut, where many workers were severely injured, that Strobridge and his men fully realized that what lay ahead of them would not only be backbreaking but would also pose unprecedented dangers. Strobridge, in fact, learned it all too well. While he was checking on his workers' progress, a premature explosion sent sharp slivers of rock into his face. For the rest of his life he was forced to wear a patch to cover the eye that was rendered useless in the accident.

It took until March 1865, almost a year, for the work at Bloomer Cut to be completed. But once it was done, the CP crews were ready to resume their climb to the top of the Sierras. That meant laying their tracks up almost five thousand feet of elevation. It meant blasting through more rock, bridging several gorges, and cutting their way through several towering pine forests before the summit of the mountains could be reached. And their reward for their achievement was an obstacle even greater than they had faced at Bloomer Cut. Looming before them was a mammoth sheer-faced cliff that rose more than 2,200 feet above the American River. The cliff had long ago been named Cape Horn after the dangerous tip of South America where so many sea travelers had lost their lives. Now, as Strobridge and his construction foreman gazed upon it, they realized that it could well be a dead end, preventing any further progress through the mountains.

A Central Pacific supply train makes its way through Bloomer Cut. It took months of digging by hand to complete the long, deep passageway.

Cape Horn was three miles long. No tunnel could possibly be built through it. Workers would have to carve a shelf all around the side of the cliff, wide enough for a roadbed upon which tracks could be laid. For this to be accomplished, huge portions of the cliff above where the roadbed was to be constructed would have to be blasted away.

But how was that to be done? Workers would have to be lowered by ropes down the sheer vertical face of the cliff. Then, while hanging precariously hundreds of feet in the air, they would pound holes into the granite and place black blasting powder and fuses inside them. As Strobridge knew all too well, nothing like this had ever been done in America. No wonder *Van Nostrand's Engineering Magazine* would later declare that "good engineers considered the undertaking preposterous."

The undertaking may have been preposterous, but standing at Cape Horn, there were men who firmly believed that it could be done. As Strobridge was considering his next step, one of the Chinese foremen came up to him and said that he and his men could do it. It might never before have been tried in America, he admitted, but back in China their ancestors had used the same tactic to build towering mountain fortresses. If Strobridge would send for straw so that his men could weave waist-high baskets, wide enough for a man to stand in while he was placing the blasting powder, they would get it done. Strobridge, who at this point was willing to try anything, immediately sent to San Francisco for straw. When it arrived, the Chinese wove the same kind of baskets that their cliff-hanging ancestors had used more than two thousand years ago. Then they inserted eyelets into each of the baskets' four sides for the ropes that would be used to lower the baskets down the face of the cliff. Knowing how dangerous their task would be, they painted good-luck symbols around each of the eyelets.

The baskets were woven to hold one Chinese worker each. When the worker was ready, men holding ropes that had been looped around a tree lowered him in his basket. When he reached a section of the face of the cliff that needed to be blasted away, he signaled for the lowering to halt. Then, swaying and scraping against the side of Cape Horn in his basket, he hammered and chiseled a hole about one foot deep into the cliff. Then he inserted the blasting powder and a fuse into the hole. As he lit

Chinese workmen were involved in every stage of the Central Pacific's operations, from the laying of the first tracks to the completion of the great iron road. Here, laborers ride a handcart to their next work site.

the fuse, the workman signaled frantically for the men holding the ropes above to pull him up and out of the range of the explosion that was about to erupt. Although most made it up safely, an untold number were unable to escape the blasts or were struck by huge chunks of flying granite and catapulted to their deaths in the deep river valley below.

For years after the great iron road was completed, trains would stop at Cape Horn so that passengers could experience what many regarded as the most spectacular view on the entire cross-country route.

It was the greatest display of courage that even the most veteran engineers among Strobridge's crews had ever seen. And day by day it continued until enough of the cliff had been blasted away to permit the carving out of a roadbed wide enough to accommodate two trains traveling in opposite directions.

THE RAILROAD AND THE CIVIL WAR

OF ALL THE AMAZING THINGS about the building of the transcontinental railroad, arguably the most astounding of all was that its first two years of construction took place at the same time that the United States was being split apart by the most devastating and tragic war in its history. In 1863, when the Central Pacific laid down its first tracks, signaling the beginning of the construction of the railroad that would change the nation forever, the North and the South were already in the third year of a conflict that would see brother fight against brother and, in some cases, father fight against son. The war would claim more than 650,000 American lives.

Along with his great desire to see the nation linked by rail, one of the main reasons President Abraham Lincoln authorized the building of the great iron road during such extreme times was that he had no idea how long the war would go on and he viewed the transcontinental as a means of quickly moving Union troops to western areas of the conflict. He also realized that tons of military supplies could be transported to war zones over the great railway more efficiently than ever before.

Today it seems extraordinary that at the same time that tens of thousands of Northern and Southern soldiers were losing their lives in places like Chancellorsville, Gettysburg, and Antietam, the Central Pacific was focused on making its way through seemingly impenetrable mountains and the Union Pacific was preparing to make its assault on the seemingly endless American Plains.

The connection between the Civil War and the transcontinental railroad did not halt when the conflict finally ended in May 1865. The thousands of veterans of the war who, after leaving the battlefields to join the ranks of both the Union Pacific and the Central Pacific, could boast not only that they had contributed immeasurably to the building of the road that linked America, but that they had taken part in the two greatest events of their time.

By the spring of 1866, the roadbed around Cape Horn had been completed and most of the tracks had been laid. Witnessing what the Chinese workers had accomplished, one reporter wrote, "They were a great army laying siege to Nature in her strongest citadel. The rugged mountains looked like stupendous ant-hills. They swarmed with Celestials, shoveling, wheeling, carting, drilling and blasting rocks and earth."

No one was more impressed with what the Chinese men had accomplished than Strobridge. He proclaimed that they were the best workers in the world and that there was nothing, no matter how difficult or dangerous, that he would hesitate to ask them to do.

And within weeks, Strobridge would ask the Chinese workers, who by this time made up more than 80 percent of the Central Pacific's workforce, to tackle an obstacle that would make what they had achieved at Cape Horn pale in comparison. From the beginning, it had been determined that more than a dozen tunnels would have to be constructed before the Central Pacific could complete its tracks through the Sierras. Only then could it make its way to the flatlands of Nevada and step up the pace in its race against the Union Pacific.

The longest of these tunnels would have to be gouged out through a peak called the Summit. This granite monster stood 7,032 feet above sea level. The tunnel needed to be a staggering 1,659 feet long and 20 feet high. In all the years that it would take for the great iron road to be built, neither the Central nor the Union Pacific would face a greater challenge than the construction of the tunnel that was called both the Summit Tunnel and Tunnel Number 6.

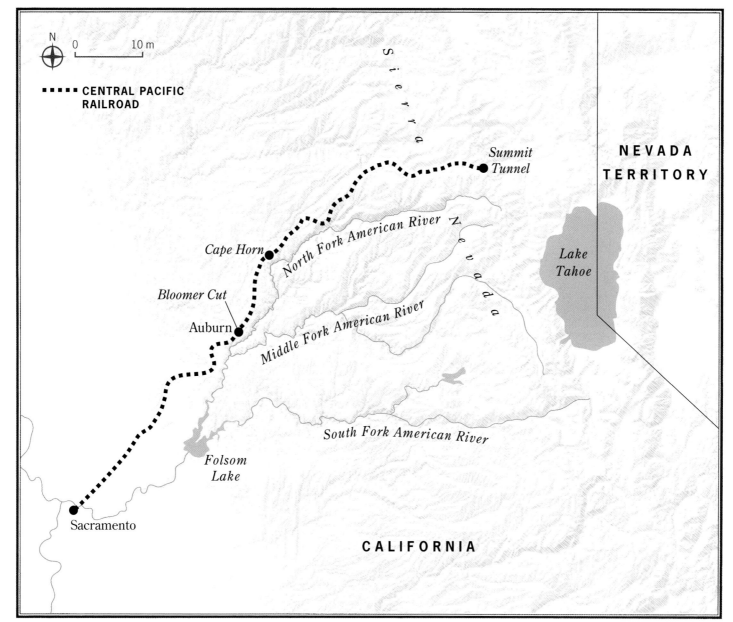

N

0 10 m

▪▪▪▪▪ CENTRAL PACIFIC
RAILROAD

Sierra

Summit
Tunnel

NEVADA
TERRITORY

Cape Horn

North Fork American River

N e v a d a

Lake
Tahoe

Bloomer Cut

Auburn

Middle Fork American River

South Fork American River

Folsom
Lake

Sacramento

CALIFORNIA

Digging the massive Bloomer Cut on the way up to the summit of the Sierra Nevada began in April 1864 and took the Central Pacific almost a year to complete. Work at Cape Horn occupied the CP from September 1865 to the spring of 1866. Meantime, CP crews had been working on the Summit Tunnel since October 1865.

It was an extraordinary undertaking. It would require not only the physical efforts of thousands of men laboring day and night but also the vision and knowledge of an engineering genius. No other railroad engineer had ever been called upon to complete such a task. Fortunately, for the Central Pacific it had such a man: Lewis Clement.

At the time the Central Pacific began laying its tracks, it took six months or more for horses and wagons to make their way through the Sierra Nevada. It is no wonder that many people believed that building a railroad through them was impossible.

LEWIS CLEMENT

BORN IN THE TOWN OF Niagara-on-Lake, Ontario, Canada, on August 12, 1837, Lewis Metzler Clement knew from an early age that he wanted to be an engineer. As a seventeen-year-old engineering student at Montreal's McGill University, he showed such promise that, in addition to his studies, he was given a position on the construction of the Montréal Water Works. When he graduated from McGill, he became a member of the engineering team responsible for the construction of Canada's huge Welland Canal, connecting Lake Ontario and Lake Erie.

In 1802, seeking new adventure, he left Canada and headed for California. It did not take long for him to find more adventure that he could have imagined. In Sacramento he was introduced to Theodore Judah, who was looking for someone to help him refine the route he had plotted through the Sierras and to help get the Central Pacific's tracklaying operations under way. Immediately impressed with the young Clement, Judah hired him on the spot.

For the better part of the next year, Judah taught Clement all he knew about railroad engineering. Clement learned so quickly and so well that eventually he was put in charge of some of the most challenging and remarkable railroad-construction projects ever attempted, including laying the tracks around treacherous Cape Horn, designing and supervising the construction of the Summit Tunnel, and conceptualizing and supervising the building of the miles of snowsheds that protected the Central Pacific's tracks in the mountains.

Clement would continue to perform what have been called "triumphs of the first magnitude in engineering" for the CP until the day the company linked its rails with those of the Union Pacific. By this time, there was no question in anyone's mind that Lewis Clement had established himself as one of the true fathers of the transcontinental railroad.

Lewis Clement looks at one of the CP's mammoth showsheds.

To construct the tunnel, Clement and the engineers who assisted him decided that a shaft would be sunk from the top of the Summit to where it was to be built. As many men as could effectively labor in the terribly cramped space would be lowered down the shaft in shifts. Since hammering and blasting away at the granite would be slow going, it was also decided that the work would go on nonstop, night and day. Dust-covered men labored with pickaxes, shovels, and prying bars. Up to three hundred kegs of blasting powder had to be carefully lowered down the shaft every day. Crammed close together and laboring by dim torchlight, the workers set explosions that caused deafening concussions of sound. It was painstaking work. The granite they were attacking was so hard that their pickaxes and chisels continually became blunt and had to be replaced. Their steel drills had to be given new edges by company blacksmiths every two hours. Despite their relentless efforts, they could manage to progress only about seven inches a day.

Frustrated by the agonizingly slow progress, Strobridge hired a crew of Welsh hard-rock miners who had been working in Nevada's gold and silver mines. The Welsh were well known for their skill at working underground. Strobridge put them to work at one end of the tunnel and ordered the Chinese laborers to work at the other end. Week after week, the Chinese cut away far more rock than the Welshmen did. Angered and embarrassed by being so outperformed, the Welshmen finally quit the project.

Now Strobridge was more frustrated than ever. From the beginning, he had never lost sight of the fact that no matter what challenges were encountered, he was not only supervising the building of an extraordinary railroad but was also engaged in an intense race with the Union Pacific. Was this race going to be lost even before this one tunnel was completed? More determined than ever to speed up the work, he devised an even more drastic plan. Aside from the slow pace with which the rock inside the tunnel was being cut away, two other things were holding up progress.

A worker poses outside the emerging Summit Tunnel. The granite through which the tunnel had to be carved was so strong that a block of it the size of a business card could support the weight of a thirty-six-ton locomotive.

One was the necessity of hauling up the granite chunks that had been cut away by hand. The other was the equally time-consuming task of lowering the heavy timbers needed to shore up the tunnel, also by hand.

Strobridge's dramatic new plan was to bring a steam locomotive up the mountain trails from where the Central Pacific's tracks currently ended to the top of the diggings. Once in place there, the locomotive's powerful steam engine could be used to raise the debris and lower the timbers. But could it be done? The twelve-ton engine would have to be dragged up more than seventy-five miles of steep, twisting mountain trails. Several early attempts failed miserably. Then a mule driver named Missouri Bill offered his services. He could do it, he claimed.

Strobridge and his foremen were doubtful at best, but they all agreed that it was worth a try. Missouri Bill, on the other hand, had no doubts. First, he stood by as the *Sacramento,* the first locomotive that had ever appeared in California, was stripped down to its heavy engine. Renamed the *Blue Goose,* it was placed on a specially designed wagon with two-foot-wide wooden wheels. Then, with ten yokes of oxen, Bill started off on his improbable mission. Cursing and yelling at the oxen all the way, he led them up the daunting mountain trails. One of his greatest challenges was the sudden appearance of horse-drawn wagons coming down the mountain. The horses became terrified at the sight of Bill's huge metal cargo and bolted. He then had to send men ahead to put blinders on any other approaching horses before they too could be spooked by Bill's unlikely caravan.

Aside from the sheer effort of climbing the mountains with a twelve-ton load, the greatest trials took place when steep downgrades were encountered. The only way that Missouri Bill could keep the engine-toting wagon from picking up speed and crashing into the oxen was to put wooden blocks under the wagon's wheels every few feet until the downslope was successfully navigated. It was a slow process, one that also had to be employed when a particularly steep upgrade was encountered.

But for six full weeks, despite it all, Missouri Bill plugged on. And he made it. In late May 1866, the *Blue Goose* stood atop the digging site on the Summit. Within days, the new hoisting engine was hauling up debris and lowering timbers faster and more efficiently than had been thought possible. And there was another important result. As historian John Hoyt Williams has written, "The old engine, snorting the soot and steam of the Sierra's first pollution, gave notice to all that the Central Pacific would not be halted by either geography or geology."

4

A WILD EXCURSION

Back out on the plains, the Union Pacific had no such formidable geography or geology to slow it down. And it was making remarkable progress. By May 1866, its construction crews had laid more than twice the miles of tracks than the UP had set down in the more than two years before Casement and Dodge had been hired to the project.

By now, the building of the transcontinental had become the nation's biggest story. Every newspaper from San Francisco to Boston sent correspondents to the work sites. Casement's army was being followed by an army of writers.

Among them was a reporter for the *Philadelphia Bulletin*. "It was," he wrote, "worth the dust, the heat, the cinders, the hurrying ride, day and night, the fatigue and the exposure, to see with one's own eyes . . . this army of men marching on foot from Omaha to Sacramento, subduing unknown wilderness . . . surmounting untried obstacles, and binding across the broad breast of America the iron emblem of modern progress and civilization. All honor, not only to the brains that have conceived [this railroad] but to the indomitable wills, the brave hearts and the brawny muscles that are actually achieving the great work."

Other than the progress of the road, the journalists had another big story to tell. Railroad service was not going to wait until the transcontinental was completed. As soon as tracks were laid between one destination and another, trains began rolling between the two points. The once empty

plains were now filled not only with the sounds of hammering and drilling and workmen's shouts, but with the sound of the new symbol of the age: the locomotive. Less than a week after the rails were laid through Kearney, Nebraska, a *New York Times* reporter stood amazed as the first train from Omaha rolled in. "And tomorrow," he wrote, "shall see the first eastward bound train! Yet already the road has been built two miles further on. This in one day!"

Increasingly, the first thing many readers turned to in their newspapers was any story that carried the dateline "End of the Tracks." One of the most interesting stories had to do with a twenty-one-year-old rifleman named William F. Cody. According to various "End of the Tracks" reports, when certain of the UP crews found themselves running short of beef, Cody had been hired to go out and shoot buffalo to supply meat to them.

He had quickly come back with more meat than the workmen could possibly eat. Only then did they learn that, young as he was, Cody was already becoming a legend for his buffalo-shooting skills. Soldiers traveling with the construction crews told them of the time Cody had astounded them by slaying eleven buffalo with just twelve rapid-fire shots. Although the workers did not realize it, they had employed a man who was to become one of America's greatest folk figures.

A wagon train filled with supplies arrives at the Union Pacific's end of tracks. A remarkable forty carloads of supplies were needed for every mile of track that was laid.

Buffalo meat was not the only addition to the UP workers' diet. One day, when Grenville Dodge returned to camp, he asked the cook where he could find two men named Rawlins and Dunn, with whom he wished to speak. The cook told him that they had heard there was a giant grizzly bear in the area and had gone out to try and shoot it so they could all have bear meat for dinner. "It was but a short time," Dodge would later write, "until we heard two shots and in a few minutes afterwards we saw Rawlins and Dunn coming towards us with the greatest speed. I knew then they had shot at the bear and had wounded him and he was following them. As Rawlins and Dunn came up I saw the bear was close and I drew the bear's attention giving me a very good shot, but I hit him a little too far back, but did not stop him. [The cook] waited until he got him face-to-face and then shot him between the eyes and dropped him. He was one of the largest grizzlies I ever saw."

By the end of the summer, Casement's workforce, spurred on by a whole new development, was moving across the plains faster than ever. In a startling and totally unexpected move, Congress had lifted the restriction that stated that the Central Pacific could lay its tracks no farther than 150 miles beyond the California-Nevada border. Now the CP was allowed to lay as many rails as it could until its tracks and those of the Union Pacific came together. Suddenly, the building of the transcontinental railroad had become more than the greatest construction enterprise the United States had ever undertaken. It had become the greatest of all races, one that would be intensified not only by the amount of money to be gained with each mile of track laid, but by the egos of men like Charles Crocker and James Strobridge and Tom Durant and Jack Casement, men determined that it would be a race that they would not allow their company to lose.

BUFFALO BILL

WILLIAM FREDERICK CODY, eventually known by millions of people as Buffalo Bill, was born on the Iowa prairie in 1846. He was only eleven years old when he went to work as a messenger for a wagon-freight company. Two years later, he went mining for gold, and he was only fourteen when he answered an ad for "skinny, expert riders willing to risk death daily" and joined the Pony Express.

During the Civil War, Cody became a scout for the Union army, where he astounded his superiors with his riding and shooting skills. According to his own accounts, he earned the nickname "Buffalo Bill" by killing 4,280 head of buffalo in seventeen months.

When the transcontinental railroad was completed, Cody returned to the army, where he earned further acclaim as chief of scouts for the Fifth Cavalry. He performed so heroically that he was awarded the Congressional Medal of Honor. It was a time when small books called dime novels were extremely popular. Beginning in 1869, Ned Buntline, the most widely read writer of these publications, created a "Buffalo Bill" series. The stories he wrote were a mixture of amazing facts and romantic fiction, and they made Buffalo Bill as great a folk hero as Davy Crockett, Daniel Boone, and Kit Carson. But Buffalo Bill's greatest fame was still to come.

Cody was a born showman, and in 1883, he organized *Buffalo Bill's Wild West*, an outdoor extravaganza that dramatized many of the aspects of frontier life that had captured worldwide attention—a buffalo hunt, a Pony Express ride, the robbery of a stagecoach, a re-creation of Custer's Last Stand. Among the stars of the show were Cody himself as "Buffalo Bill," the woman sharpshooter Annie Oakley, and the famous Native American chief Sitting Bull.

For more than thirty years *Buffalo Bill's Wild West* played to enormous audiences throughout the United States and Europe. By the time it was over, William Cody had become one of the most famous people in the world.

A man of boundless energy, Cody played a major role in founding the town of Cody, Wyoming, in 1895. There, along with opening a hotel, he established the TE Ranch, which eventually grew to some 8,000 acres and ran more than 1,000 head of cattle. Cody also opened a dude ranch and a big game hunting business.

Cody made a fortune from his show business and ranching successes but lost all of it due mainly to bad investments. He died on January 10, 1917, and is buried in a tomb blasted from solid rock at the top of Lookout Mountain near Denver, Colorado.

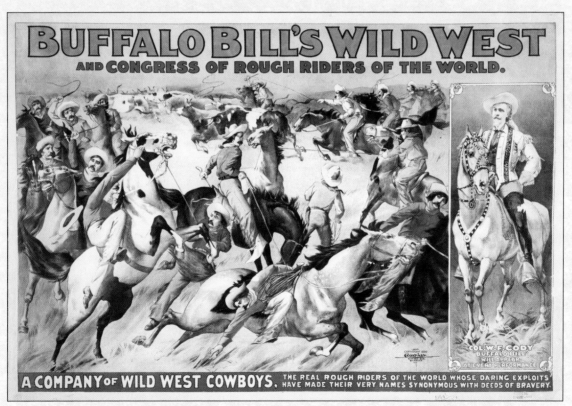

Buffalo Bill, shown at the right of this poster for his extraordinarily popular show, would always acknowledge that it was his accomplishments as a buffalo hunter for the Union Pacific that launched him into fame and fortune.

From the time that both the Central Pacific and the Union Pacific had begun laying their tracks, each company had hired individuals to secretly check on the other's progress. Encouraged by its spies' reports of the difficulties the CP was having in the mountains, the UP pushed its advantage, hired scores of additional graders, and sent them one hundred miles ahead of the tracklayers. Grenville Dodge, determined to outdistance the Central Pacific as much as he could before it broke out of the Sierras, packed up his surveying equipment and set out for Wyoming to plot a final route through the Rockies.

At the end of its tracks, Casement's crews stepped up the pace as never before. "Wonderful indeed," *New York Herald* reporter Henry Stanley wrote, "is the rapidity with which . . . the roads [are] graded, ties laid down, and the rails secured to their places by the railroad-makers. Squads of Irishmen under energetic taskmasters, are scattered all along working with might and main."

In early October 1866, the Union Pacific's tracks reached the 100th meridian of longitude, 247 miles west of Omaha. It was both a milestone and an occasion for celebration. And for Thomas Durant, it was something more. Despite this great achievement, the UP had a major problem. It was seriously short of funds. New investors were needed as quickly as possible. Now, in the 100th-meridian achievement, Durant saw a golden opportunity to attract donors to the Union Pacific. It was also, he believed, a chance to gain huge publicity for the UP. He decided to celebrate the accomplishment by inviting specially selected individuals and their families to take part, at the UP's expense, in an excursion to the 100th meridian. It was to be a party. But not just any party. Durant was determined to make it an extravaganza, something that people would never forget.

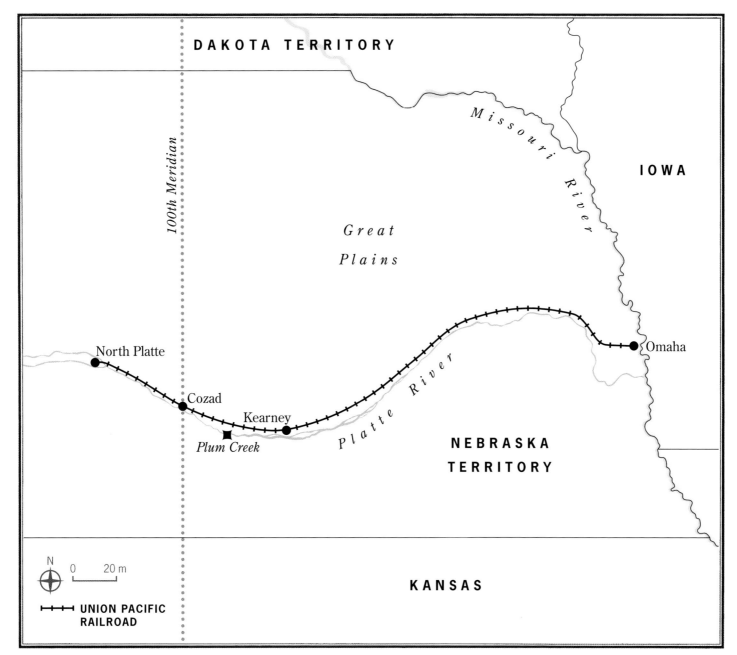

DAKOTA TERRITORY

Missouri River

IOWA

100th Meridian

Great

Plains

North Platte

Omaha

Cozad

Kearney

Platte River

Plum Creek

NEBRASKA

TERRITORY

N

0   20 m

KANSAS

┣━┿━┿━┿━┫ UNION PACIFIC
RAILROAD

The Union Pacific crews were working at such a peak of efficiency when they crossed the 100th meridian of longitude that they hardly took note of the event. In little more than a week, the end of the UP's tracks was forty miles farther westward.

He began by inviting more than three hundred of the nation's most influential people—congressmen, cabinet members, leaders of business and industry. Among the more than two hundred who accepted the invitation were Rutherford B. Hayes, future president of the United States; Robert Todd Lincoln, son of the martyred president; French noblemen; a Scottish earl; and, to Durant's delight, a large number of millionaires. Along with inviting reporters from every one of the country's major newspapers, Durant also hired two photographers to record each of the several days' events he had planned. He topped it all off by acquiring a portable printing press and hiring a newsman to publish a daily account of the excursionists' experiences.

In mid-October, those who had accepted Durant's invitation assembled in New York City. From there they were taken by train to Saint Louis, where they boarded two elegant steamboats that Durant had leased to take them to Omaha, where the extravaganza would culminate. Throughout the two-day voyage, they were treated to the music of two

separate bands. A magician was on hand to entertain them. There were even two barbers present to trim the mustaches, sideburns, and whiskers of the gentleman guests.

The highlight of the trip, however, was the dinner that was served on the first night out. The excursionists were people used to elegance. And they were no strangers to opulence. But none had ever experienced anything like the meal that, for three hours, was set before them. For the occasion, Durant had hired one of Chicago's most famous chefs and directed him to prepare the most exotic array of dishes he could. The chef did not disappoint. Aside from the various soups, gumbos, and appetizers that led off the meal, the excursionists were served six kinds of boiled meat, seven varieties of roast meat, ten types of cold meat, and twenty-nine different main courses. They included dishes of duck, venison, wild turkey, rabbit, and quail. Pyramids of candies, fruits, and other desserts also were part of the menu.

Somehow, all the guests survived the gluttonous meal and the dancing that followed. On October 22, they arrived in Omaha, where they were given a tour of the facilities the Union Pacific had erected there. The excursionists gazed in wonder at the roundhouse that could shelter twenty huge locomotives, the two-story machine shop, the blacksmith shop that contained a dozen forges, and the long car shops where UP mechanics and craftsmen were producing some ten railroad cars a week. Durant made certain that the employees conducting the tour emphasized how facilities like these were prime examples of the strength of the UP, the bright future it had in front of it, and how wise it would be for an individual to invest in the company.

THE MIGHTY LOCOMOTIVE

"TYPE OF THE MODERN—emblem of motion and power—pulse of the continent." That's how the famed American poet Walt Whitman characterized the locomotive. And it was highly publicized events like Thomas Durant's excursion to the 100th meridian that emblazoned the locomotive in the national consciousness.

The Central Pacific locomotives that made their way through the Sierra Nevada and across the Nevada desert, and the Union Pacific locomotives that left their billowing trails of smoke across the American plains were made possible by one of the world's greatest developments—the harnessing of steam power. The first workable steam engine was invented in 1712 by the Englishman Thomas Newcomen. It was used mainly for pumping water out of flooded British coal mines. Newcomen's invention was not efficient enough to be used for transportation purposes, but in the late 1700s, James Watt, now regarded as the father of the steam engine, came up with a series of inventions, including pressure gauges and steam regulators,

A steam locomotive, c. 1865. Far more than any other mechanical device before it, the locomotive changed America and the world.

that paved the way for the use of steam power in locomotives. In 1802, British inventor Richard Trevithick created the first steam-powered engine that could propel locomotives along rails. In February 1804, after the first trial run of his invention, Trevithick reported that he had transported seventy men and about ten tons of iron approximately nine miles on a trip that took four hours and five minutes. But this was too long a time to capture the public's imagination, so Trevithick's invention did not catch on. In 1814, however, the first practical steam locomotive was built by Englishman George Stephenson and his son Robert. In 1825, the Stephensons gained further fame when they established the Stockton and Darlington Railway, the first public railway line for steam locomotives. They followed up this success when they built their now-famous steam locomotive the *Rocket,* which attained the unheard-of speed of twenty-nine miles per hour.

The first American steam locomotive was built in 1825 by John Stevens, who demonstrated its use on a circular track in his backyard in Hoboken, New Jersey. The first locomotive to operate on an American railroad was the *Stourbridge Lion,* which was shipped to America from England. Like other British locomotives that followed, the *Stourbridge Lion* was too heavy for the relatively light and often uneven American tracks and was soon put out of service. In 1830, the distinction of being the first American locomotive to pull a passenger car on a railroad went to Peter Cooper's *Tom Thumb*. Although it was small, the *Tom Thumb* was powerful enough to convince the directors of the newly formed Baltimore and Ohio Railroad to use only steam locomotives on their line. In 1831, a giant leap forward was taken when E. L. Miller's *Best Friend of Charleston* became the first locomotive to pull a train of cars on an American railroad. The *Best Friend* was in service for almost six months, until its driver, annoyed by the sound of its hissing steam, shut down a safety valve, causing an explosion that destroyed the locomotive and killed him.

Despite this disaster, American manufacturers soon came to dominate locomotive building. By the end of the 1800s, one company alone, the Baldwin Locomotive Works, was turning out six hundred locomotives a year. Nowhere in the world was the locomotive more visible than on the transcontinental railroad. American philosopher Henry David Thoreau spoke for millions of his fellow citizens when he proclaimed, "When I meet the [locomotive] with its train of cars moving off in planetary motion . . . with its steam cloud like a banner streaming behind . . . it seems as if the earth has got a race now worthy to inhabit it."

The next day, the main attraction began. Accompanied by the two bands, more than two hundred excursionists set out for the 100th meridian. The nine-car train in which they traveled was led by two smoke-belching locomotives decorated with deer antlers and American flags. Most of the excursionists rode in four newly made passenger cars adorned with thick carpets and heavy, elegant drapes. Members of Congress and other particularly important guests were seated in a specially constructed parlor car that had chairs upholstered with silk. Durant had reserved the most special car of all for himself, his family, and his friends. It was called the "Lincoln Car." The late president had never ridden in it while he was alive, but it was the car that had become famous for having carried his body in his funeral train. The last three cars of the train that one reporter would call "the most sumptuous and resplendent, not only in America, but all over the world," included a gentlemen's smoking and drinking car, a "cooking car," and a car that held baggage and supplies.

Durant had planned the train trip west as carefully as all the events that had preceded it. When the excursionists arrived at their first stop, they were greeted by a roaring campfire and a collection of tents in which they were to spend the night. They got their first surprise immediately after supper was served. As they were gathered around the campfire, a group of Pawnee Indians, their faces covered in war paint, suddenly appeared and began a tribal dance. Their whoops and cries frightened many of the guests, including one woman who fainted when one of the Indians danced near her. Durant calmed the excursionists by explaining that he had paid the friendly Pawnees to stage the "entertainment."

The next day began with Durant offering the male guests the choice of taking part in either a buffalo or an antelope hunt. Once this adventure

Durant's guests became truly frightened when Pawnee Indians staged a pretend raid on the excursion.

began, the excursionists-turned-hunters could not believe how many buffalo and antelope they came upon so quickly. What they didn't know was that Durant had also staged this event. He had paid professional guides to round up great numbers of the animals so that his guests would have an easy time bagging their trophies. No record has been found as to what was done with the animals that fell prey to yet another of Durant's shenanigans.

Directors of the Union Pacific meet under the sign Durant had erected to mark the UP's arrival at the 100th meridian. Although most of the UP's directors despised Durant's often shady tactics, they could not deny that under his leadership the railroad was making great progress in its race against the Central Pacific.

Once the two-hour "hunt" was over, the journey resumed, and late that afternoon the train reached the 100th meridian. Durant had told Casement to expect his group of excursionists and urged him to have his men working as furiously as they could for the benefit of the guests. But when they arrived at the anticipated spot, all that was there was a large sign that read: 100TH MERIDIAN, 247 MILES FROM OMAHA. Casement was quite willing to put on a show for the visitors, but he was not going to halt his progress waiting for them. By the time the excursion train had reached the meridian, the UP crews had moved forty miles farther down the plains.

Immediately, Durant had the excursion train move on to where the end of the tracks now stood. Then, after leaving the train, the excursionists looked on in awe as Casement's men laid down more than eight hundred feet of track in less than thirty minutes. The day ended with the guests proudly having their pictures taken with the workers.

That evening, as the excursionists got ready for the return journey to Omaha, they made a group decision. They decided to issue a formal declaration publicly thanking the Union Pacific

for making the excursion available to them. They also wanted to let the world know what an extraordinary thing the UP was accomplishing. They expressed their feelings with a formal resolution:

WHEREAS, An excursion party of ladies and gentlemen, from various places in both hemispheres, started from New York City on the evening of October 15, 1866, to visit the Union Pacific Railroad as far as finished, to a point west of the hundredth meridian of west longitude, and

Whereas, Said excursionists, with many others who have joined them on the route, have this day reached said destination at a point on said railroad two hundred and seventy-five miles west of Omaha . . .

Resolved, That this excursion party, here assembled in the center of this vast continent, now offer up our heartfelt gratitude and thanks to Almighty God for His manifold blessings, among which we enumerate . . . a Union unbroken and indestructible, with all the material resources necessary for the comfort of mankind in a high and rapidly advancing state of development, and with a vast net-work of railroads and telegraphs, essential not only to our national prosperity and the interests of all our people, but also to the civilization and commerce of the world, including, among the most important of them all, that vast work — the Union Pacific Railroad.

Resolved, That it is the deliberate opinion of this excursion party that our nation and the world have abundant cause to rejoice that the Union Pacific Railroad was projected and is in successful progress to completion, and we now congratulate mankind at the success of this magnificent enterprise.

Resolved, That our thanks are due and hereby tendered to the Union Pacific Railroad Company, for their energy and enterprise in the rapid construction of their railroad, as well as for this excursion.

It was a magnificent testimonial, particularly, as far as Durant was concerned, coming from so many people in the position to either politically support or invest money in the Union Pacific. One of Durant's concerns had been that some of the excursionists, particularly those from the West Coast, while enthusiastic supporters of a transcontinental railroad, might be more inclined to invest in the Central Pacific than the UP.

During the return journey to Omaha, Durant had the engineer stop the train. Inviting his guests to disembark, he led them on a more-than-two-hour tour of one of the most fascinating phenomena of the plains—an enormous prairie-dog town. His guests shook their heads in both wonder and amusement as thousands of animals popped their heads out of their holes and then just as quickly retreated back inside them.

Still, Durant was not done. Farther down the tracks, he again ordered that the train be halted. As the sky became brilliantly illuminated, the excursionists peered out the windows at what even those who had lived in the West all their lives regarded as the most spectacular sight the plains had to offer—a roaring prairie fire. It was awesome, it was thrilling, and it was more than a little bit frightening. And it, too, had been deliberately staged by Durant.

When the excursionists returned home, they could talk of little else than the wonders of the "Wild West" and what the UP was accomplishing in the wilderness. Some, like engineer and politician Silas Seymour,

Beyond the 100th meridian, Casement's army kept moving at a record pace. "It's hard to realize," declared the New York Times, "that so great a distance may be accomplished in so short a time."

went a bit overboard. Writing of the excursion, he described it as "the most important and successful celebration of the kind that has ever been attempted in the world." What pleased Durant most was that many of the excursionists did just what he had hoped for and became Union Pacific investors.

But it wasn't only the political figures and the wealthy businessmen on the trip who made the excursion such an overwhelming success. Along with his desire to attract needed funds and increased political support for the UP, Durant had hoped that the excursion would bring the company favorable publicity. And without exception, the reporters from the nation's most important magazines whom Durant had invited wrote stories not only describing the wonders of all they had experienced but also portraying the Union Pacific as a company acting heroically in the interests of the American people. Proclaiming that the UP's march across the plains was as great an achievement as the Union's triumph in the recent Civil War, the *Cincinnati Gazette* declared, "There is nothing connected with the Union Pacific Railroad that is not wonderful." Responding to statements like these, people across the nation purchased millions of dollars' worth of Union Pacific bonds.

The great excursion had served its purpose more than even Durant had dreamed. Thanks to both the glowing endorsements and the funds it received, he could not help but feel that the Union Pacific had gained a leg up in a race with the Central Pacific that now promised to become even more intense.

5

TUNNELS, SNOW,
AND
NEVADA AT LAST

The Central Pacific had received the news that it was now free to lay its tracks as far as the eventual linking site with obvious joy. But by the winter of 1866, one thing was absolutely clear. Up to this point in this great race, the Union Pacific had been blessed with far more good fortune than the CP. While Durant had been staging his extravagant celebration, the Central Pacific was still struggling to complete its Summit Tunnel. Although the use of the *Blue Goose*'s engine to haul up debris and lower timbers had helped move the work along, the agonizingly slow pace of cutting away the faces of the tunnel continued. Then Mother Nature suddenly played her hand.

Winters in the Sierras were always severe. But no one had ever witnessed anything like what took place in the winter of 1866–1867. Forty-four blizzards struck the mountains. One of these storms lasted thirteen consecutive days without an hour of letup. Drifts surrounding the Summit Tunnel piled up forty feet high. "These storms," one observer wrote, "made the road impassable even for sleighs. . . . The snow when new fallen is very light, so that a man without snowshoes would sink to his waist or shoulders. Into this the oxen would flounder, and when they lay down, worn out, [they could] be roused [only] by . . . twisting their tails."

Remarkably, the work on the tunnel went on. "The Chinese," historian Thomas W. Chinn, founder of the Chinese Historical Society of America, wrote, "lived practically entirely out of sight of the sky that Winter, their shacks largely buried in snow. They dug chimneys and air shafts and lived by lantern light. They tunneled their way from the camps to the [entrance to] the tunnel to work long underground shifts. A remarkable labyrinth developed under the snow."

Despite the perseverance of the Chinese workers, progress on the Summit Tunnel continued at a snail's pace. It was a situation that James Strobridge simply could not abide. All too aware that if the Central Pacific was to be a real contender in the race with the UP, it had to get out of the mountains, he decided to take his most dangerous gamble. He was aware that as recently as 1860 a powerful new explosive had been developed. It was called nitroglycerine. Strobridge had heard stories of how accidental explosions of the chemical had demolished a Central American steamship and blown up half a block in downtown San Francisco. He had, however, also been told by construction engineers who had tried it on their projects that it was at least twice as effective as blasting powder.

The photographer titled this image "Laborers and Rocks Near Opening of Summit Tunnel."

It was more than tempting. But did Strobridge dare use it, especially when the unstable chemical would have to be transported to the tunnel over jarring mountain trails? He was still making up his mind when he was informed that a Scottish chemist named James Howden was on the West Coast and that he had the ability to mix the chemicals that created nitroglycerine right at the tunnel site. Strobridge quickly sent for Howden and put him to work making his powerful explosive.

At first it seemed as if a miracle had been wrought. Instead of the small amount of granite that the black powder blasted away, nitroglycerine tore away huge sections of the rock. And it not only tore the rock away; it pulverized it, leaving far less debris to be removed. In addition, unlike black powder, it produced no tunnel-filling smoke that choked those men working in the cramped quarters. Thanks to nitroglycerine, work on the rock faces progressed more than two feet a day rather than a few inches.

Strobridge and his engineers were delighted. Nitroglycerine had proven that its reputation for effectiveness was well founded. But as great progress on the tunnel continued to be made, the nitroglycerine proved to be as dangerous as it was reputed to be. Week by week, Chinese workers were killed in blasts set off when their pickaxes accidentally struck the granite face near where the explosive had been set. Others were killed when the volatile chemical exploded much sooner or much later than intended.

Finally, Strobridge had to admit that the nitroglycerine was just too dangerous. They had to stop using it and go back to black powder. By this time, however, greater progress had been made on the tunnel than Strobridge or any of his foremen could have hoped for only a few months ago. And then, at four o'clock in the afternoon of August 28, 1867, as noise from yet another black powder explosion was still reverberating, beams of light shone into the tunnel. Gaping at the light, the workmen could see that it was coming from the torches of graders working through the night in advance of the tunnel. They had broken through. The Summit Tunnel had been conquered.

Wiring the welcome news back to Central Pacific headquarters, Lewis Clement exclaimed, "Perseverance alone [has] conquered." It was an achievement that could not be overestimated. Clement, Strobridge, the Chinese workmen, and their foremen, working by hand under impossible conditions, had, in thc words of a later observer, "created one of the greatest moments in American history."

Filled with relief at having put the most backbreaking and dangerous days of the Summit Tunnel building behind them, Strobridge's men looked forward to completing the conquest of the mountains. But then their old enemy winter struck again.

Some of the workmen actually turned the newly fallen snow into sport. "These storms were grand," engineer John Gillis proclaimed, as both Irish and Chinese workers tried to move about on long strips of wood that they were told the Norwegians called skis. Skiing had not yet been introduced into America, but ski-clad workmen began racing one another down the slopes.

The welcome amusement, however, was short-lived. The snows kept coming, the drifts piled up to incredible heights, and before long, Gillis had a very different kind of story to tell. "Snowslides or avalanches were frequent," he wrote. "The storm winds being always from the southwest, form drifts or snow-wreaths on the northeast crests of hills. Then these become too heavy, which is generally towards the close of the storms, they break off, and in falling start the loose snow below. This slides on the old crust. Near the close of one storm, a log house with a board roof, containing [fifteen or sixteen workers] was crushed and buried up at daybreak. . . . Towards evening a man coming up the road [could not find the house] and alarmed the camp, so that by six o'clock the men were dug out."

The men in the house could count themselves among the lucky ones. In another enormous snowslide, twenty men died when the flimsy barrack in which they lived was carried clear down the mountain. Their bodies were never found. No one will ever know how many workers simply vanished when struck by other avalanches. "There was constant danger,"

The snows that hit the Sierras in the winter of 1867–68 were, in many places, even deeper than those of the previous, record-setting winter. This was the scene at the Central Pacific Railroad Depot in Cisco, California, elevation 5,911 feet.

one railroad historian wrote, "for as snows accumulated on the upper ridges, avalanches grew frequent, their approach heralded only by a brief thunderous roar. A second later, a work crew, a bunkhouse, an entire camp would go hurtling at a dizzy speed down miles of frozen canyon. Not until months later were the bodies recovered; sometimes groups were found with shovels or picks still clutched in their frozen hands."

Once again, the CP's work was on the verge of being halted. But even with the snow in the ravines and canyons piled up as high as sixty feet, Strobridge was determined to get out of the mountains. Here, in the winter of 1867, as he had done the previous winter, he ordered the men to cut snow tunnels between their barracks and the work sites. "Some of these tunnels," engineer D. O. Mills reported, "were more than two hundred feet long."

SKIING

THE CENTRAL PACIFIC WORKERS who startled onlookers by racing down the Sierra Nevada slopes on skis were engaging in an activity as old as antiquity. Archaeologists have determined that the oldest known skis, found in Russia near Moscow, date back to 6300 BCE. Rock carvings in Bøla, Norway, that were created in 4000 BCE include depictions of men using skis. And ancient records reveal that skiing was so revered in the Scandinavian countries of Norway, Sweden, and Denmark that the Vikings worshipped Ullr and Skade as the god and goddess of skiing. Records also disclose that in the Middle Ages, skis were regularly used by Scandinavian hunters, warriors, and farmers. According to other documents, by the 1700s units of the Swedish army both trained and competed on skis.

The first skis used in America were brought by Norwegians who had immigrated seeking to strike it rich in the California goldfields. It is more than likely that the CP transcontinental railroad workers who took advantage of the 1866 Sierra snows to don skis were men who had been recruited from the gold mines. According to *Sierra Heritage* magazine, by the 1880s, a network of ski trails connected the many gold-mining camps and were regularly used by doctors and mail carriers. One of these mail carriers was Granville "Zack" Zachariah, who, according to *Sierra Heritage,* was "a stunner . . . he comes up over the crest of the Enterprise ridge . . . and before I can wink he scoots down into Bloody Run, leaving a trail of feathery snowflakes in his wake like a tail of a comet."

For at least the next half century, skiing in the United States was largely confined to the region where Zachariah had made his mark. But the introduction of newer and easier-to-use skis, more effective bindings, and various types of waxes designed to make skis go faster led to the beginnings of nationwide popularity.

Perhaps the greatest development of all took place in 1936, at the Sun Valley ski resort, in Idaho. And it had a railroad connection. As skiing in America became more popular and as ski trails became steeper, the greatest need was to get skiers to the top of the trails. Sun Valley's founder, Averell Harriman, who, in 1936, was also the chairman of the Union Pacific, asked his UP engineers to design the nation's first ski lift. One of the engineers, James Curran, had earlier designed a continuous cable with hooks to unload bananas from ships. Curran created the same type of cable with chairs attached to the hooks; the ski lift was born, and skiing was on its way to becoming one of the nation's most popular pastimes.

Clearing snow from the tracks was an even bigger problem. At one point, Strobridge had some five thousand men engaged in nothing other than shoveling the heavy snow. But, as one CP official lamented, "it was found impossible to keep [the track] open over half the time and that mostly by means of men and shovels, which required an army of men on hand all the time at great expense."

Something other than shoveling clearly needed to be done. At the end of the previous winter, the CP, at its facilities in Sacramento, had built the largest snowplow ever constructed. It was thirty feet long, and its front end was shaped like the prow of a battleship. But even when it was pushed by twelve locomotives, the plow could not cut its way through the drifts.

Now Strobridge and Crocker were even more desperate than they had been when the seemingly impassable Cape Horn had blocked their path. They decided to try something that had never been done on any railroad in the world. Impossible as it seemed, they would attempt to put a roof over the miles of track that had been laid through the snowiest areas. "It was decided," one official later explained, "that the only positive means of protecting the road was by snowsheds. . . . Although the expense of building a shed nearly forty miles in length was almost appalling and unprecedented in railroad construction, yet there seemed to be no alternative."

Lewis Clement, fresh off his Summit Tunnel miracle of construction, was chosen to design what would be more like giant wooden tunnels than sheds, built to withstand tons of cascading snow. The CP then hired Arthur Brown, a veteran bridge builder from Scotland, to head the construction. Before the immense undertaking was completed, Brown would have 2,500 men, including hundreds of experienced carpenters, working for him.

Central Pacific workmen pose with the world's largest snowplow.

Six trains running around the clock would be required to bring timber, spikes, bolts, and other needed materials to the building sites.

Reinforced with iron braces, rods, and supports, the snowsheds were "timbered," as one observer noted, "as heavily as line-of-battle ships." Before the sheds were completed, Brown and his men used a staggering sixty-five million feet of timber and nine hundred tons of bolts and spikes. Equally staggering was the cost of the project, equivalent to more than twenty-five million dollars today.

Central Pacific carpenters construct one of the several snowsheds built to keep the heavy snows off the tracks. No similar structures had ever been built on any other railroad.

But no one, certainly not anyone connected with the Central Pacific, could argue with the fact that it was worth it. Observing the way the sheds kept the tracks clear, even during the heaviest storms, a writer for *Van Nostrands's Engineering Magazine* put it simply. "They have conquered the snow," he wrote.

They had overcome what one historian described as their "most consistent and debilitating enemy." And with that success came the prospect of at last getting out of the mountains and continuing over the flat Nevada desert. But there was still a great amount of work to be done in the Sierras, including the building of at least a dozen more tunnels. Although the greatest number of workers had been assigned to the building of the tunnel at the summit, a smaller group had begun work on the other tunnels at about the same time. And while none of the other tunnels would be anywhere near as long or as difficult to construct as the Summit Tunnel, each would present its own challenges.

Each of the tunnels had to be tall enough to accommodate the high smokestacks of the locomotives that would pass through it. Each had to be wide enough to allow two trains traveling in opposite directions to pass through at the same time. As one observer later wrote, "The approaches to all the tunnels were covered with men . . . [who] worked day and night in three shifts of eight hours each. Thus, time was saved. . . . As an illustration of the hurry, I may mention walking two miles over the hills after dark and staking out the east end of Tunnel 12 by the light of a bonfire. At nine o'clock the men were [still] at work."

They would continue working nonstop until all the tunnels were completed. As far as Strobridge was concerned, he would leave the supervision of their remaining labors to various of his foremen. He simply could not

The snowsheds were not the only structures the Central Pacific erected to keep heavy snows off the tracks. Here, a carpenter works on a snow galley, a shed-like structure bolted to cliffs near the rails and designed to keep rocks as well as snow from falling upon the tracks.

wait to tackle the Nevada desert, where he was certain he would make up for the time spent in the mountains. "It was necessary," Strobridge would later write, "to have the heavy work [in Nevada] done . . . in advance of the main force; and 3,000 men with 400 horses and carts were sent to that point, a distance of 300 miles in advance of the track. Hay, grain and all supplies for these men and horses had to be hauled by teams over the [Nevada] deserts . . . for that great distance, there being no supplies to be obtained on the entire route."

At the same time, construction boss Crocker was engaged in an undertaking that would, when completed, be regarded by many as one of the greatest feats of all. Three huge locomotives and forty cars loaded with tons of rails, spikes, and other materials needed to lay the tracks across the first portions of Nevada sat perched in the mountains. They had to be disassembled and taken over the summit, across snow-covered trails, and into Nevada.

"We hauled locomotives over," Crocker would later recount, "and when I say we, I mean myself. We hauled them on sleighs. . . . we hauled some of them over on logs, because we could not get a sleigh big enough. After the Iron Horses and their tenders and cars were brought slipping and sliding down the slope, they had to be loaded onto wagons . . . and dragged along a rough and muddy road. . . . After this was done, a cavalcade of sleds and wagons followed with [the tons of supplies]."

At the same time that Crocker was getting the vital supplies out of the mountains and Strobridge was overseeing his army of graders in Nevada, CP tracklayers had begun making their descent down the Sierras' eastern slope. On December 13, 1867, jubilant Chinese workers set down the first rails across the Nevada line.

SETTING A STANDARD

ALTHOUGH THE WORK of the graders and the tracklayers was much more commonly known, the labor of another group for both the Central Pacific and the Union Pacific was every bit as essential. They were the gaugers, men who, as soon as tracks were laid, made certain that they were exactly the right distance apart to accommodate the wheels of the trains that would be traveling on them.

In 1830, George Stephenson designed England's Liverpool and Manchester Railway, the world's first twin-track passenger railroad. He had set his rails four feet, eight and a half inches apart, based on the width of the coal wagons of the day. This width between the rails came to be called the Stephenson gauge. In 1846, the British Parliament passed an act by which the Stephenson gauge became the standard gauge for all railroads built in England.

Because England had pioneered railroad building, a significant number of American engineers went there to study railroad construction. Many of the early American railroads built by these engineers used the Stephenson gauge. However, the Charleston and Hamburg railway line was constructed with a five-foot gauge. When nearby states began to build railroads to connect with the Charleston and Hamburg, they copied this gauge. By 1861, more than seven thousand miles of track with this wider gauge had been laid in the South.

There were various reasons why some railroads turned their backs on the Stephenson gauge. Some believed that using a unique gauge size would prevent rival companies from connecting to their line. After the United States invaded Canada in the War of 1812, railroads in Canada were built with a five-foot, six-inch gauge to prevent American trains from using Canadian tracks.

As more people and freight traveled significant distances by train, often transferring from one line to another, it became essential that rail gauges be standardized. Despite the considerable cost involved, almost all American railroad companies adopted the Stephenson, or standard, gauge. So, too, did Canadian railroads. The Central Pacific and Union Pacific, however, had no need to convert. From the time they began building the transcontinental railroad, both companies faithfully adhered to the Stephenson gauge.

News that the Central Pacific had succeeded in laying tracks through the mountains quickly spread. Soon, the first train ever to carry passengers through the dense, towering Sierras made its way to a hastily erected temporary depot near the California-Nevada border. For the train's passengers, it was a thrilling experience. For the laborers who had made it possible, it was a most rewarding sight. "[The Chinese worker] with his patient toil," wrote one observer, "has broken down the great barrier [of the Sierras] at last and opened over it the greatest highway yet created for the march of commerce and civilization."

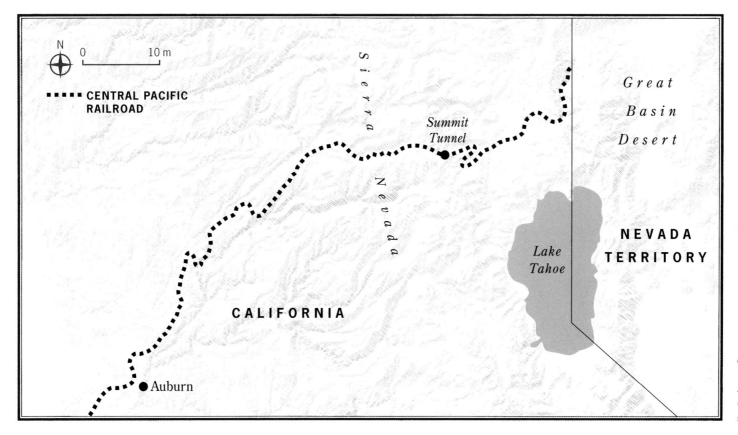

The Central Pacific finally broke through the Summit Tunnel on May 3, 1867. By mid-December 1867, CP crews had worked their way to the Nevada border.

6

HELL
ON
WHEELS

Back on the Great Plains, Jack Casement's army was continuing what seemed to be an uninterrupted march westward. It had extended its rails to North Platte, Nebraska. Then, with little warning, the UP's good fortune finally ran out. A succession of blizzards hit the plains. "We are out of luck in this country," a UP engineer wrote. "Wind blowing and snow drifting . . . half the men either blind or frozen, looks bad." The UP workmen went through what their Central Pacific rivals had endured for the past two winters. Conditions became so bad that Casement halted work. All through February and March 1866, his crews were held prisoner as the snow continued to fall.

Like many of his workers, Jack Casement regarded the building of the transcontinental as the greatest of adventures. He would be involved in constructing railroads until the day he died.

Finally, in April, the weather changed dramatically. The snow stopped falling, and what had already fallen started to melt, and work resumed. Frustrated by the delay, Thomas Durant became more determined than ever to keep up or even better the pace Casement and his men had established before suffering their first real setback. "I will pledge myself," he telegraphed a congressman, "to complete two miles a day for the first one hundred working days after the frost is out of the ground."

Casement was only too happy to take up the challenge. He both increased the pressure on his men and never stopped pushing himself. "[I] never saw a man you worked harder for," Casement's wagon driver later wrote. "Many times we drove 24 hours, changing horses, and when I [became exhausted] Jack drove."

Casement was not the only one pushing himself to the limit. Grenville Dodge was equally driven. He was everywhere—following the tracklayers, checking on the progress of the grading crews far ahead of the rails, traveling farther ahead on horseback to see how the surveyors were progressing. And the man who had been the first to determine the UP's cross-country route westward was back to doing his own surveying, sometimes more than a hundred miles in advance of the rest of the construction army.

In July 1867, Dodge had traveled ninety miles north of Denver, Colorado, the only substantial community in the Rocky Mountains, seeking out the best path for the UP's tracks once they reached that far west. Aware that he was in an area that provided easy access to the rich coalfields of the Dakotas, Dodge founded a town in what a year later would become Wyoming Territory that he named Cheyenne, for the Native American Cheyenne nation. Actually, Dodge had an even more important reason for founding Cheyenne than its proximity to coal and other mineral deposits. He was convinced that as the Union Pacific pushed farther and farther westward, it needed a place not only where trains traveling in all directions could converge but also where facilities to build and service these trains, like those in Omaha, could be erected. This place, he predicted, "is to be the depot for all posts north and south and also the distributing point for all points in Colorado. . . . [The Union Pacific] shall also build a large workshop, machine shops, round houses, etc." Dodge's belief that Cheyenne would become a thriving town was quickly verified when thousands of people began to pour into the site, intending to build permanent residences.

Back at the tracks, Casement and his men were continuing their march across the plains. Mercifully, there had been no more blizzards, although they were certain that once they reached the hills and mountains at the

After laying tracks over hundreds of miles of flat prairie land, the Union Pacific finally reached the mountainous terrain of the West. Here, Union Pacific workers shape the heavy timbers that will be used to shore up one of the first tunnels they need to construct.

distant ends of the plains, they would have to battle the snows again. And they were equally certain that they would be in danger from the native peoples whose lands they were crossing.

They were right, although the killing would begin not with the Indians but with the whites. On November 29, 1864, a U.S. cavalry regiment of some seven hundred men led by Colonel John Chivington, a man yearning to gain military glory for himself, attacked and destroyed a peaceful Cheyenne village at Sand Creek in Colorado Territory. Over 150 Cheyenne were murdered, two-thirds of whom were women and children.

Thirty-nine days later, more than one thousand Sioux, Arapaho, and Northern Cheyenne warriors attacked the town of Julesburg, Colorado, in retaliation, killing a great number of civilians and soldiers. The Indians then continued on through the Platte Valley, tearing down whatever telegraph poles and wires they encountered and destroying several stage coach stations.

In his memoir, Grenville Dodge would remember how these two serious raids and a number of other incidents marked the beginning of ongoing conflict between the Indians and the railroad workers. "Our Indian troubles," Dodge would later write, "commenced in 1864 and lasted until the tracks [were joined]. . . . I remember one occasion when they swooped down on a grading outfit in sight of the temporary fort of the military some five miles away and right in sight of the end of the track. The Government Commission to examine that section of the completed road had just arrived, and the commissioners witnessed the fight. The graders had their arms stacked [next to where they were working]. The Indians leaped from the ravines and, springing upon the workmen before they could reach their [weapons], cut loose the [horses and mules] and caused a panic."

It was a serious incident, carried out by people whose way of life was being increasingly threatened with every mile of track that was being laid. The Plains Indians "were defending their lands," historian Donald Fixico would state. "Anyone would defend their lands, their homelands."

Hundreds of miles ahead of the tracks, Arthur Ferguson and his fellow surveyors continued to have encounters with Native Americans. "May 22 [1867]," Ferguson's diary reads. "The Indians have killed four men. When the men go to work, even if they are in full sight of the camp, they go well armed." Fearful of the effects such statements would have on Casement's men, Durant made sure the workers didn't hear them.

What Durant could not keep hidden, however, was what took place on August 7, 1867. Alarmed by how far the railroads had moved into their territory, a Cheyenne chief named Pawnee Killer decided he had had enough. Led by Pawnee Killer, forty Cheyenne warriors swooped down on the tracks near Plum Creek, Nebraska. Attacking the rails, they bent them and then removed the spikes that held them down. Then they waited, hoping a train would make an appearance. They were not disappointed, and when the train hit the severely damaged section of the tracks, its engine overturned, killing its engineer, its fireman, two brakemen, and three telegraph repairmen who were aboard.

The carnage was not over. Soon another Union Pacific train came barreling down the tracks, crashed into the wreckage of the first train, and overturned. The Cheyenne Indians then killed eight people and set fire to both trains.

The events of Plum Creek caused enormous concern among the construction crews, even those men who were only two years removed from having taken part in some of the fiercest Civil War battles. A small contingent of United States soldiers had accompanied the Union Pacific crews across the plains. Now UP officials telegraphed the military, pleading for a great many more soldiers to protect the workers. But even before they arrived, Casement would not let the attacks slow the pace of the tracklaying. If anything, over the next three months he drove the men even harder, prodding them on to two- and even three-mile tracklaying days. And, on November 13, 1867, the UP's tracks reached Cheyenne.

Even before Casement's construction train made its appearance, thousands of people in Cheyenne raced to the spot where the rails were being laid. "Our citizens swarmed along the grade, and watched with most intense delight and enthusiasm, the magic work of track-laying," exclaimed the *Cheyenne Leader*. "The hearty greeting we all gave this gigantic enterprise, so rapidly approaching, was too deep and full for expression. There was no shouting and cheering, but one full tide of joy that sprung from the deep and heartfelt appreciation of the grandeur of the occasion and the enterprise, and that bright future now dawning on the remote regions of the far west."

The completion of the tracks through Cheyenne itself engendered an even greater response, one to which the *Chicago Tribune* devoted almost an entire front page. "Yesterday, at 5 o'clock in the afternoon," the *Tribune* reported, "track-laying on the UP was completed to the city of Cheyenne, and in a few moments the whistle of the locomotive was heard above the noise of the hammers and the rattle of wagons all over the bustling city." The *Tribune* made a special point of describing how Cheyenne's entire population "rushed wildly to the railroad track," where there was a huge banner proclaiming, "Honor to whom honor is due; Old Casement we honor you."

A UNIQUE PROCLAMATION

GRENVILLE DODGE was right in predicting that Cheyenne had a bright future. Within four months of its founding, it grew to a population of four thousand. And its citizens were a distinct kind of men and women who, for the most part, sought to escape the constraints and formalities of the established cities. To let the world know why they had settled in Cheyenne, the men of the town prepared a document explaining their reasons.

First they listed those characteristics of city life that they were purposely avoiding by settling in Cheyenne:

> 1st. Extravagant dress, requiring one to two changes . . . each day.
> 2nd. Late hours for meals and sleep.
> 3rd. Restriction of speech.
> 4th. Too dainty and delicate food.
> 5th. Too little exercise.
> 6th. Too much dust and heat.
> 7th. Too [many expensive stores].

Then they listed the privileges they received living in Cheyenne:

> 1st. The most simple dress, consisting of flannel shirts, overalls . . . top boots with spurs, and slouch hat.
> 2nd. Early hours, breakfast at 4 a.m., and sleep at 8 p.m.
> 3rd. Perfect freedom of speech on all subjects.
> 4th. Plain, simple and healthy food, consisting of bacon and hard-tack with a judicious sprinkling of antelope, black tailed deer, elk, prairie dog, speckled trout, and mountain sheep.
> 5th. Exercise on horseback with carbines and revolvers, from fifteen to thirty miles per day, Sundays and 4th July excepted. . . .

And generally, to do just about as we please at all times and under all circumstances, with due and gentlemanly respect to our companions, and a proper observance of the laws of Nature and Nature's God, which reign supreme throughout all this vast and beautiful country. . . .

Although we are now so far from the Westerly confines of civilization, we expect within a few short months to be broken in upon by the shrill whistle of the locomotive upon the Great Union Pacific Railroad, which is now making such rapid progress through these beautiful plains.

Cheyenne's Union Depot. The arrival of the Union Pacific's tracks transformed Cheyenne into a major community.

The article concluded with words that epitomized the UP's march across the plains: "Before nightfall," it stated, "Cheyenne was left half a mile in the rear." As the tracks moved on, no one in the crowd would have argued with the newspaper's final statement. "Cheyenne," it read, "is now connected with Chicago and the rest of mankind."

By April 1868, the Union Pacific's tracks were more than thirty miles west of Cheyenne. Having been told that the Central Pacific was now making greater progress than ever, Casement had his men working on Sundays, for which he paid them double wages. He had also lengthened the construction train to eighty cars. More bunk, dining, and kitchen cars had been added, as well as a bakery car, a car that carried feed for the horses and mules and also housed a saddle shop, and a telegraph and pay-roll car. And by this time, some five thousand infantrymen and cavalrymen had been deployed along the UP's route to protect the workers.

In mid-April, Casement's crews reached the first of the mountain ranges they would encounter in the far west. Their days of laying rails over the flat American plains were over. They had covered the plains with more than 985 miles of track. And they had left more than rails behind them. Whenever the construction crews stopped for a period of time to lay their tracks, a town would spring up almost overnight. These towns became one of the most intriguing aspects of the building of the iron road. They were not ordinary settlements. Because they were the wildest, most lawless communities the United States had ever known, they were called Hell on Wheels towns. And almost every one of them would be abandoned as quickly as they appeared.

On the open, barren plains, there were no places for the thousands of rough and rowdy railroad workers to find entertainment. There were no places for them to spend the money they received each payday. But there was no shortage of people anxious to relieve them of their wages. Almost as soon as the UP began to trek across the plains, these towns, with their hastily erected, flimsy wooden buildings, shacks, and large tents, appeared. And they immediately attracted all kinds of unsavory characters—outlaws, scoundrels, gamblers, hoodlums—each intent on getting their share of the UP laborers' money.

In many ways, the railroad workers were a perfect target for those who set up in the Hell on Wheels towns. The UP workmen were themselves hardly a quiet, peaceful lot. They were hard-drinking, boisterous men, many of whom loved a good brawl. Many of them had served in the Union army during the Civil War. They were used to guns, gunfire, and taking huge risks. Most were not fazed by the chaos and danger that lurked in every Hell on Wheels town. Many actually welcomed them.

One of the first of these temporary towns to pop up was Sidney, Nebraska. When the earliest passenger trains (put into service after a significant number of miles of track had been laid) made a stopover there, travelers were not allowed to leave the train for fear of being shot. It quickly became clear that even remaining in the trains while in Sidney was not safe. Several instances were reported of inhabitants of the town peppering trains with bullets while terrified passengers ducked for cover.

North Platte, Nebraska, the place where the UP had been stranded during the 1867 blizzard, was even worse. "Every gambler in the Union seems to have steered his course here," *New York Herald* reporter

Henry Stanley wrote. "Every house is a saloon and every saloon is a gambling den. Revolvers are in great requisition." After passing through North Platte, an army major gave his own description of what he saw there. "At North Platte," he wrote, "they were having a good time gambling, drinking, and shooting at each other."

As bad as things were in North Platte, the town was peaceful when compared to Julesburg, on the Nebraska-Colorado border, which, during its brief existence, became known as the "Wickedest City in America." "I . . . believe," Stanley reported, "that there are men here who would murder a fellow creature for five dollars. Nay, there are men who have already done it, and who stalk abroad in daylight unwhipped of justice. Not a day passes but a dead body is found somewhere in the vicinity with pockets rifled of their contents." Like almost all other Hell on Wheels towns, Julesburg disappeared almost as quickly as it had been set up. Within three months of its founding, it was abandoned, joining the ranks of America's growing number of ghost towns.

Wherever the Union Pacific crews set up a construction site, a town would materialize. Western travel writer Samuel Bowles followed the building of the Union Pacific over much of its route, through miles of the most desolate parts of the nation. To him, no Hell on Wheels town emerged in a more desolate or inhospitable locale than Benton, perched in the middle of nowhere in the Wyoming Territory. Describing Benton, Bowles wrote, "This congregation of scum and wickedness was . . . called Benton. One to two thousand men, and a dozen or two women were encamped on the alkali plain in tents and board shanties; not a tree, not a shrub, not a blade of grass was visible; the dust ankle deep as we walked through it, and so fine and

Few of the rowdy citizens of Julesburg could have predicted that the town would have such a brief existence.

volatile that the slightest breeze loaded the air with it, irritating every sense and poisoning half of them; a village of a few variety stores and shops, and many . . . [liquor] shops; by day disgusting, by night dangerous; almost everybody dirty, many filthy . . . averaging a murder a day."

Within two months, as the construction crews moved on, Benton was gone. Disappearing with it were those who had inhabited it. "Like its predecessors," Bowles wrote, "[Benton] fairly festered in corruption, disorder and death, and would have rotted, even in this dry air, had it outlasted a brief sixty-day life. But in a few weeks its tents were struck, its shanties razed, and with their dwellers moved on fifty or a hundred miles [down the tracks] to repeat their life for another brief day. Where these people came from originally; where they went when the road was finished, and their occupation was over, were both puzzles too intricate for me."

Many of those whose migrations so puzzled Bowles had moved on to Bear River City, another site in the Wyoming Territory, a place destined to experience, at least in one instance, even more violence than Benton. Things got so out of hand in that lawless community that a vigilante committee of concerned citizens was formed. In the vigilantes' first encounter with some of those who were terrorizing the town, three of the lawbreakers were shot and killed. Intent on revenge, a large mob of Bear River City's worst elements staged a riot, later vividly described in *Crofutt's Trans-Continental Tourist's Guide:* "The Bear River City Riot cost sixteen lives," the publication stated. "The mob first attacked and burned the jail, taking thence one of their kind who was confined there. They next sacked the office and destroyed the material of the *Frontier Index* [newspaper]. Elated with their success, the mob, numbering about 300 well-armed desperados,

GAMBLING ALONG THE RAILS

JUST AS THE Union Pacific laborers were inviting targets for the professional gamblers who inhabited the Hell on Wheels towns, so too were the passengers who rode the trains along the transcontinental line and other smaller western railroads. It is estimated that more than three hundred professional gamblers rode the trains of the Union Pacific alone. Gambling on the trains became so commonplace that a deck of cards became known as a railroad bible.

The most skilled of the gamblers may have been Alice Ivers. A colorful character who often smoked cigars while playing cards, she was also quite beautiful and did not hesitate to use her good looks to distract the men she gambled with. Most of all she was an extraordinarily talented poker player. By the time her days gambling aboard the trains were over, she had earned the nickname Poker Alice and had relieved passengers of more than three million dollars in today's currency.

Another gambler, George Devol, became well known for another reason. Like many of the professional gamblers in the Hell on Wheels towns or aboard trains, Devol relied on cheating in his card playing. He had begun his gambling days on Mississippi riverboats, where he had learned such dishonest tactics as secretly marking cards and hiding cards up his sleeves. What made Devol notorious was that although he won a great deal of money through his cheating, he was also caught at it a good many times. Newspapers of the day contain stories of Devol leaping from a speeding train in a hail of bullets fired by an enraged passenger he had just cheated.

Another notorious train-riding gambler, Canada Bill Jones, had been George Devol's partner during the time they were cheating Mississippi riverboat passengers. Jones, who focused his gambling on a card game called three-card monte, became best known for attempting to legitimize his illicit activities. Told that the Union Pacific was about to crack down on gambling on its trains, Jones offered the UP a deal. He would pay the company ten thousand dollars if, in return, he was given the exclusive one-year right to play three-card monte with passengers on the trains. Hoping to clinch the deal, Jones promised to target only traveling salesmen and Methodist preachers. But, as railroad historian Keith Wheeler has written, "with a sorry lack of sporting spirit, the UP turned him down."

Street scene in Bear River City. Like almost all the Hell on Wheels towns, Bear River City—or Bear Town, as it was also called—was abandoned as abruptly as it had been erected.

marched up the main street and made an attack on a store, belonging to one of the leading merchants. Here they were met with a volley from . . . rifles, in the hands of brave and determined citizens, who had collected in the store. The mob was thrown into confusion and fled down the street, pursued by the citizens, about thirty in number. The first volley and the running fight left fifteen of the desperados dead on the street. The number of wounded was never ascertained, but several bodies were afterwards found in the gulches and among the rocks, where they had crawled away and died. One citizen was slain in the attack on the jail."

Hell on Wheels towns would continue to follow the Union Pacific's progress all the way to its tracks' completion. The towns would be characterized by the same atmosphere that prevailed in Julesburg and Benton. Commenting on the situation in newly formed Corinne, Utah, the very last Hell on Wheels town, the *Deseret News* stated, "This place is fast becoming civilized, several men having been killed there already."

7

TRACKS ACROSS THE DESERT

James Strobridge and Charlie Crocker had been waiting for the day they would begin leading their crews across the flat Nevada landscape. But what they quickly discovered was that setting down rails in Nevada meant meeting the challenges of a vast and uninhabitable desert. It meant toiling in a region described by one early traveler as "a purely arid plain, covered with sage brush, varied by white alkali flats, holding but little water and that bad; with hot springs here and there; lizards and jack rabbits the principal inhabitants: [land with] absolutely no timber." It meant coping with conditions as different as possible from those they had endured in the mountains.

In the Nevada desert, the workers were forced to haul their heavy rails, wield their huge sledgehammers, and lug wheelbarrow after wheelbarrow in temperatures that rose to 120 degrees Fahrenheit. Water was transported in huge wooden tanks on flatcars and had to be conserved. Just as Cape Horn and the Summit Tunnel had taken their human toll, the Nevada desert would exact its own price. Hundreds of workers collapsed on the line, and scores of others came close to death from heatstroke and dehydration.

With the mountains behind them, Strobridge would allow no slowdown in the work. This was the opportunity to make up for lost time, the chance to lay down more miles of track than the Union Pacific. As one astounded observer, gazing at the activity around the CP's construction train, wrote, "Long lines of horses, mules and wagons were standing in the open desert near the camp train. The [livestock] was getting its breakfast of hay and barley . . . . Foremen were galloping here and there on horseback giving or receiving orders. Swarms of laborers, Chinese, Europeans and Americans were hurrying to their work. On one side of the track stood the moveable blacksmith shop where a score of [blacksmiths] were repairing tools and shoeing horses and mules. . . . To the west were the rails . . . stretching back as far as the eye could reach. To the eastward stretched the grade marked by a line of newly distributed earth. By the side of the grade smoked the camp fires of the blue clad laborers who could be seen in groups waiting for the signal to start work. These were the Chinese, and the job of this particular contingent was to clear a level roadbed for the track. They were the vanguard of the construction forces. Miles back was the camp of the rear guard—the Chinese who followed the track gang . . . finishing the roadbed."

As this photograph reveals, there could be no greater contrast in terrain than between the mountains through which the Central Pacific had laid its tracks and the flat, barren desert it was about to cross.

Aside from the frenzied activity, something else was taking place in Nevada as well. "As I was moving my outfit forward . . . after having been placed in charge as Engineer of Construction on the building of the road eastward from the California-Nevada State line," Joseph M. Graham later wrote, "I measured and staked out what was later to be the city of Reno." It would be the first of a number of communities that, thanks to the CP, would eventually blossom in the desert.

To the Central Pacific workers laboring in the scorching desert heat, there was a type of train as important to them as the construction train. It was the life-sustaining water train that followed them from one end of Nevada to the other.

FOUNDING RENO

RENO, NEVADA, had the distinction of being the first town founded as the Central Pacific began to make its way across the mostly barren Nevada desert. Reno's earliest development began well before the CP's graders and tracklayers appeared in the area. In 1859, the first major discovery of silver ore in the United States, known as the Comstock Lode, took place. Almost immediately after the discovery was made, Charles Fuller built a log bridge over the Truckee River, near the site of present-day Reno, and charged a toll to silver-seekers crossing over to get to the mining area. The next year, Fuller built a hotel and a restaurant.

In 1861, Fuller sold his holdings to Myron Lake, who named the spot Lake's Crossing. Some six years later, when it became clear that his property stood in the path of oncoming Central Pacific tracks, Lake saw an opportunity to increase his business prospects. Realizing that a railroad station on the site of his land would bring more people to his hotel and restaurant, he made a deal with Charles Crocker. Under the terms of their agreement, Lake gave a section of his land, large enough for the tracks to be laid upon it, to the Central Pacific. In return, the CP erected a railroad depot.

Lake was not alone in recognizing the opportunities created by a railroad operating in the vicinity of the Comstock Lode. Crocker was also convinced that any town that arose in the area, particularly one with its own depot, was bound to flourish.

No one is certain who gave Reno its name. Some claim that it was Joseph Graham, who laid it out. Others say it was Crocker. What is known is that it was named for Civil War hero General Jesse Lee Reno, who died while leading Union troops at the Battle of South Mountain. What is also true is that Crocker's belief in the future of the town was well realized and that Reno, a town carved out of the desert, not only thrived but grew into a community that today proudly calls itself "the biggest little city in the world."

By this time, the Central Pacific's Chinese laborers had become among the quickest railroad construction workers in the world. But nothing was ever fast enough for Strobridge. And in the middle of the desert, he came up with a new and quicker way of laying track by doubling both the number of men setting down the ties and the number of men fastening the rails to them, and giving them the room to do it more rapidly than ever.

Under his new system, a first group of workers placed every other tie. This group was immediately followed by a second gang of tie setters who placed the rest. Once the tracklayers set the rails on the ties, a first gang of spikers drove in every other spike. They were quickly followed by a second group of spikers who completed the spiking job. To save more time, Strobridge came up with yet another strategy. Whenever his crews came to a ravine or other obstacle that called for the time-consuming task of building a bridge, he had them skirt the area by laying their tracks in snakelike curves, often for miles around it. It was a strategy that particularly pleased the CP's directors. Every extra mile of track laid meant more money in their pockets.

Thanks in great part to Strobridge's new measures, the Central Pacific, for the first time since laying its initial rails, was moving forward as quickly as the Union Pacific had in crossing the Great Plains. Two- and three-mile tracklaying days became common. In July and August 1868 alone, forty-six miles of track were laid, inspiring an *Alta California* reporter to write, "[The tracklaying site] that knew [the CP] in the morning knew it no more at night. It was nearly 10 miles off . . . while a smooth, well-built, compact road bed for traveling stretched from the morning site to evening [stopping] place." A San Francisco newsman was equally impressed. "Taking out my watch," he wrote, "I timed the last half mile I saw laid, and it took a little less than 28 minutes."

For Strobridge and Crocker the race against the Union Pacific became an obsession. They drove their crews on relentlessly until tracks lined the desert as far as the eye could see.

From September to the end of December 1868, the CP's crews continued setting rails at the same rapid pace they had established after Strobridge had begun driving them across Nevada. By the end of 1868, they had, in that year, laid almost 370 miles of track. The Central Pacific was now at the Utah border.

The men of the Union Pacific were also racing toward the Utah line. After working their way over almost a thousand miles of mostly flat terrain, they were about to encounter something totally different. They had reached Sherman Summit, which sat atop the vital pass Grenville Dodge had discovered in 1865 while fleeing from a band of Native Americans. Dodge had named it for his friend and former military colleague William T. Sherman. At an altitude of 8,640 feet, it was more than a thousand feet higher than the peak through which the Central Pacific had constructed its Summit Tunnel.

The Sherman Summit may have been higher, but fortunately for the UP, it presented none of the challenges that the Central Pacific had faced in making its way through the Sierra Nevada. There was nothing like Cape Horn around which the CP had to build an unprecedented type of ledge to hold its tracks. There was nothing like the monstrous granite peak through which the Central Pacific had constructed its Summit Tunnel.

By April 16, 1868, Casement's men had succeeded in laying their rails through what would be not only the highest point on the transcontinental railroad but the highest of any railroad in the world. Among those most impressed with the feat was a writer employed by the Union Pacific. "Sherman is gained," he wrote, "and the traveler stands . . . as near heaven

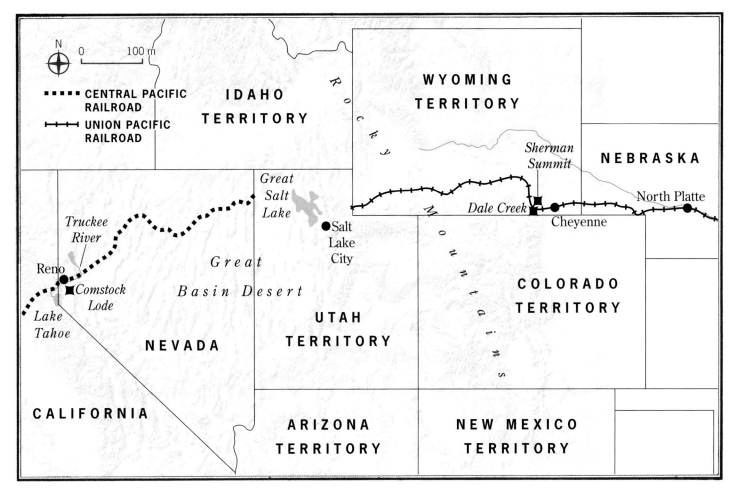

as the Union Pacific Railroad approaches. The rarefied atmosphere allows the blood to course freely through the veins; the spirits rise . . . the eye is ravished . . . the senses are astonished. . . . Here the waters of the continent divide. In one direction, [they] start on their long journey to the Atlantic; in the other, they tumble down the Pacific slope."

WILLIAM TECUMSEH SHERMAN

WILLIAM TECUMSEH SHERMAN, the man for whom Sherman Summit was named, stated that the building of the transcontinental railroad would require the "work of giants." And Sherman would turn out to be one of the greatest giants of them all by providing more moral and physical support for the railroad's construction than anyone outside the rail companies.

In 1849, as a young army lieutenant, he conducted the only survey seeking a possible railroad route through the Sierras. But Sherman received almost no recognition for this preliminary survey. Twelve years later, however, he would begin to gain enormous fame as a Union general in the Civil War.

In 1862 and 1863, as a Union general, Sherman served under Ulysses S. Grant and played a key role in the capture of the Confederate stronghold at Vicksburg. In 1864, after taking command of all Union

forces in the western theater, he led his troops on a march that resulted in the capture of Atlanta and its railroad yards, a decisive turning point in the war.

After the Civil War ended, Sherman remained in the service, and in 1869, when Grant became president of the United States, he succeeded him as commanding general of the army. He remained in that post until 1884.

His support for the transcontinental railroad remained strong throughout his years at the top of the Union army command. Sherman arranged for Grenville Dodge's release from the army so that he could become a driving force of the Union Pacific. He persuaded his brother, who was a U.S. senator, to foster and promote legislation in support of the transcontinental. And beginning in 1868, he posted more than five thousand soldiers along the tracks to protect the railroad workers from Indian attacks.

To celebrate his company's having built the highest railroad in the world, Tom Durant traveled all the way from New York to help set the final rail. The UP leader was so pleased with the achievement that he could not resist sending a telegram to CP president Leland Stanford, bragging about what the UP had done. Stanford wired back his congratulations, stating, "We cheerfully yield you the palm of superior elevation; 7,242 feet has been quite sufficient to satisfy our highest ambition." Stanford, however could not resist adding another line with an obvious double meaning. "May your descent be rapid," he wrote.

An even greater challenge than Sherman's Summit was faced by special work crews of Casement's army. At the same time that the rails were being laid through the Summit, UP bridge builders were engaged in one of the most treacherous and exhausting undertakings of all. At a towering canyon at Dale Creek, in Wyoming Territory, UP engineers and crews had to build a 650-foot-long bridge over the creek that flowed 150 feet below. Constructing a bridge of that length made of wood and strong enough to enable locomotives and long lines of railcars to pass over it while the ever-present Wyoming winds whipped through the canyon was difficult to imagine.

Timber for the immense structure had to be felled in the Michigan woods and shipped to Chicago, where it was cut to specifications. The wood was transported by rail across a temporary bridge over the Missouri River and then finally carried along UP's tracks from Omaha to the building site. The bridge builders were forced to risk their lives as they worked high above the canyon in strong winds on what one historian has called "a structure of interlaced toothpicks."

A Native American gazes upon the Central Pacific's tracks as the Central Pacific approaches the Utah border. To many, the transcontinental's progress was an enormous triumph, but to those who first inhabited this land, it spelled the end of their way of life.

slowed down waiting for the special water trains that ran up and down the line, they kept moving on. So rapidly, in fact, that in August alone they laid a record sixty-five miles of rail.

It was still not enough for Casement. In September, motivated by additional bonuses, his men on several occasions laid between four and five miles in a day. The work was now continuing until midnight, with evening crews laboring by the light of bonfires. Late in October, with the tops of the water barrels now rimmed with ice, the end of the UP's tracks were within a few miles of the Utah line. The two great railroad companies that had started out half a continent away from each other were now less than five hundred miles apart.

8

A RACE
FOR GLORY

No one knew better than Tom Durant that the grading work that lay ahead in Utah's hilly and rocky terrain would be difficult and time consuming. And, for the first time, UP crews would have no choice but to construct tunnels in the most challenging areas. If the UP was to win the race across Utah, it had to hire a large number of new workers. And Durant knew just where to find this army of laborers.

There were some eighty thousand members of the Church of Jesus Christ of Latter Day Saints, better known as Mormons, living in Utah. Led by a charismatic man named Brigham Young, the Mormons were known for being hard workers, just the type of people that Durant so badly needed.

THE MORMONS

THE MORMONS were a deeply religious people with a unique history. Because they held beliefs that were very different from other religions, they had from their beginnings suffered both discrimination and persecution. Seeking to find a place where they could practice their religion in peace, they had followed their leader Joseph Smith first from New York to Ohio, then to Missouri, and then to Illinois, where Smith was killed by a prejudiced mob.

Their new leader was a man named Brigham Young, and in the mid-1840s, determined to find a place so remote that he and his fellow Mormons could escape persecution, he led them on a thousand-mile trek all the way through the Utah territory wilderness, where they finally settled in a desert next to the Great Salt Lake. Because it was so dry and so seemingly unsuitable for farming, it was a place where no one else wanted to live. But the Mormons irrigated the dry land with water from creeks and streams, planted crops, and flourished. By 1860, the original Mormon pioneers had been joined by more than forty thousand other believers, and more than 150 settlements had been established.

All of this took place under the watchful eye of Brigham Young. He was a great leader. And, having experienced firsthand how difficult it was to travel across the United States, he was a great champion of a transcontinental railroad, particularly one that would carry passengers through the treacherous landscape that he and his early followers had traveled on their way into Utah. "We never went through the canyons or worked our way over the dividing ridges," he wrote, "without asking where the rails could be laid."

Young and those who had followed him into Utah would receive credit for having blazed the route into that territory. As reporter Samuel Bowles wrote once the great iron road had been completed, "But for the pioneership of the Mormons . . . all this central region of our great West would now be many years behind in its development, and the railroad, instead of being finished, would hardly be begun."

Blazing the way through the challenging Utah landscape was an invaluable contribution, and the Mormons' importance in making the transcontinental railroad a reality would grow even greater once they went to work for both the Union Pacific and the Central Pacific.

On May 6, 1868, Durant sent a telegram to Brigham Young asking him if he could supply a large number of men to work on the UP's construction project. In less than an hour, he got a telegram back from Young stating that he was willing to do so. If Durant had known what was happening within the Mormon settlements, he would not have been surprised at

Utah would be the final battleground in the race between the Union Pacific and the Central Pacific. Here, Union Pacific crew members, along with heavy rolling equipment, test the strength of a newly completed bridge.

Young's quick, positive response. During the past two growing seasons, the Mormon communities had been struck by a devastating plague of grasshoppers. The insects had destroyed so many of the Mormons' crops that thousands of their men were out of work and in desperate need of money.

Immediately after receiving Young's welcome reply, Durant sent one of his engineers, who knew the Mormon leader personally, to work out a contract with him. When it was signed, it provided that Young would supply four thousand workers whose main tasks would be grading, tunneling, and bridge building. As part of the agreement, the UP promised that from that time on, Mormons, particularly those immigrating to their settlements, would be allowed to travel on Union Pacific trains at lowered rates.

Durant had found the additional workers he needed. And he had received a bonus. For, in addition to significantly increasing the size of the UP workforce, the Mormon laborers proved to be among the most hardworking and dedicated he had ever seen. And unlike so many of the other UP workers, the Mormons, who weren't allowed to smoke, drink, or gamble, had absolutely no inclination to spend time in any Hell on Wheels towns that might spring up along the way.

Gratified to at last be earning money again, many of the Mormons actually sang as they went about their labors. A particular favorite was:

We surely live in a very fast age.
We've traveled by ox-team, and then took the stage.
But when such conveyance is all done away,
We'll travel in steam cars upon the railway!

Hurrah! Hurrah! For the railroad's begun!
Three cheers for our contractor, his name's Brigham Young.
Hurrah! Hurrah! We're honest and true,
For if we stick to it it's bound to go through.

"Stick to it" they did. By the time the work on the Utah roadbed was completed, one historian would write, "It was acknowledged by all railroad men that nowhere on the line could the grading compare in completeness and finish with the work done by the people of Utah." He meant the Mormons.

Mormon laborers would prove invaluable to the Central Pacific and the Union Pacific as the railroads sought to outdo each other in their race across Utah. Here, Mormons employed by the Union Pacific pose for the camera after completing work on a tunnel in Utah's Weber Canyon.

Not everyone was happy with what the Mormons were contributing to the UP's efforts. The Central Pacific's directors viewed their rival's new not-so-secret weapon in the great race with alarm. There was only one solution. The CP had to get its own army of Mormon workers to combat what those working for the UP were accomplishing.

No one was more determined to make this happen than CP president Leland Stanford. Traveling first by rail and then by stagecoach, Stanford made his way to Salt Lake City, where he convinced Brigham Young to supply the CP with enough workers to grade roadbeds from the Nevada border to Utah's Weber Canyon. When Young agreed, the industrious Mormons were working for both the CP and the UP.

With the hiring of the Mormon workers, both companies had successfully addressed the manpower problems that they faced in Utah. But there was another long-standing issue that simply would not go away. It was the extraordinary challenge of getting millions of tons of building materials and equipment to the construction sites. In 1869, at the same time that CP tracklayers were beginning to set their first rails on Utah soil, no fewer than thirty-five ships, carrying rails, spikes, and other supplies that would be needed in Utah, were at sea, headed for San Francisco. The equipment would then travel by train to Strobridge's crews. Included in the precious cargo were eighteen locomotives. Marveling at the situation, the *Salt Lake Daily Reporter* exclaimed, "There is not a rail on the CP line of the road that has not been brought a distance of six thousand miles."

At the same time, the UP crews were met in Utah by the heaviest snows they had encountered since those that had battered them back on the plains more than a year ago. But this time there would be no halting. Neither Durant nor Casement would allow it. Instead, promising the men double wages, they had them break up the frozen earth with pickaxes and blasting power and drag ties and rails out of snowbanks. It was exhausting work, made even more daunting when, for the next hundred miles of tracklaying, temperatures continued to hover at zero degrees or below. No one was prouder of the westward progress than Grenville Dodge. "We laid the track over the Wasatch Range [in Utah's Promontory Mountains] in the dead of winter on top of snow and ice," he wrote. "We built almost as rapidly through the winter as we did during the summer."

Meanwhile, despite the snow, Strobridge was driving his crews eastward just as hard. "Keep right on laying rails just as though you did not care for the snow," Huntington had begged him. "And if you do that I will forever pray that you will have your reward." Now the Central Pacific was also approaching the Promontory range. Only fifty miles separated the two great rivals.

Thomas Durant personally followed the Union Pacific's progress in Utah. Here, Durant (standing next to the two-person carriage on the right), along with other Union Pacific officials, visits a Union Pacific graders' camp.

WIRES ABOVE THE TRACKS

THE PACIFIC RAILWAY ACT OF 1862 was more than an act to build a transcontinental railroad. It was, as officially stated, "An Act to aid in the Construction of a Railroad and Telegraph Line from the Missouri River to the Pacific Ocean." The act also specifically stated that the telegraph lines were to keep up with the tracks every step of the way across the continent. And the men who made up the telegraph work gangs were determined to see that that happened. So much so that an intense rivalry developed between the telegraph gangs and the track gangs.

Like the laying of the rails, the erection of some two thousand miles of telegraph poles and wires was done with military precision. At the same time that wagons distributed rails along the graded earth, other wagons brought telegraph poles to the graded site. While the poles lay on the ground, one telegraph gang nailed crossarms onto them while another dug holes for the poles. Then a third telegraph gang erected the poles. Once this was completed, a wagon carrying a huge reel of wire appeared. As the wagon moved forward, the wire was uncoiled, allowing a wire gang to carry it up the pole and attach it to the insulators.

It was a precise operation but not without its challenges. As one reporter observed, "At times lack of wagons make it impossible to keep up the supply of poles, and the telegraph gangs, who pride themselves on never letting the track get ahead of them, utilize sage brush, barrels, ties—surreptitiously taken from the track—or anything else that would keep the wire off the ground until the supply of poles again equal the demand."

Throughout the erection of the transcontinental telegraph line, operations were interrupted by Native Americans who cut the line not only to interrupt the telegraph crews' progress but to get at the shiny copper wire that they found perfect for making jewelry. An even greater challenge came from another source. As historian John Hoyt Williams wrote, "Even a few dozen [buffalo] could damage track, and, later, thousands of telegraph poles would go crashing to the ground as the heavy beasts of the treeless plains discovered they made marvelous scratching posts."

Just as the building of the transcontinental railroad revolutionized transportation in America, the erection of a cross-country telegraph line provided the United States with the greatest long-distance communication system it had ever had. And the telegraph was essential to the building of the great road itself.

The construction trains of both the Union Pacific and the Central Pacific contained a telegraph car in which Jack Casement or James Strobridge or their engineers or foremen could wire for new supplies or for new groups of workers. And as the UP moved farther and farther from its home base in Omaha and the Central Pacific moved farther from its headquarters in Sacramento, it would be the telegraph that allowed both Strobridge and Casement to end each day by reporting on what progress had been made.

Telegraph workers prepare poles for the stringing of wires that, like the rails, would link the nation.

Although the Pacific Railway Act of 1862 had authorized both companies to build the iron road, it made no mention of where the tracks were to be joined. Picking such a site was a decision that the leaders of both companies kept avoiding. They were getting paid by the mile, and by 1869, it was apparent that, despite the great race in which they were involved, both would have been content to keep laying track forever. As the two lines got closer and closer to each other, their grading crews began constructing parallel roadbeds that ran for miles past each other. Also, the directors of both the CP and the UP had become masters at finding different ways to siphon money from the companies' treasuries into their own bank accounts. No wonder they didn't want construction to end.

Finally, the government had had enough. On March 4, 1869, the same day that he was sworn in as president, Ulysses S. Grant issued a stern warning to both companies. If they didn't get together and agree on the spot where the rails would be linked, the government would stop paying them until they did.

It was a threat that could not be ignored. On April 8, 1869, the Union Pacific's Grenville Dodge and the Central Pacific's Collis Huntington met behind closed doors in Washington, D.C. on April 9, after a full day of bitter argument, they agreed on a place where their tracks would meet. It was Promontory Summit, Utah, a desolate spot north of the Great Salt Lake, 690 miles from Sacramento, 1,086 miles from Omaha. The next day Congress passed a resolution officially making Promontory Summit (often mistakenly referred to as Promontory Point) the place where the "rails shall meet and connect and form one continuous line."

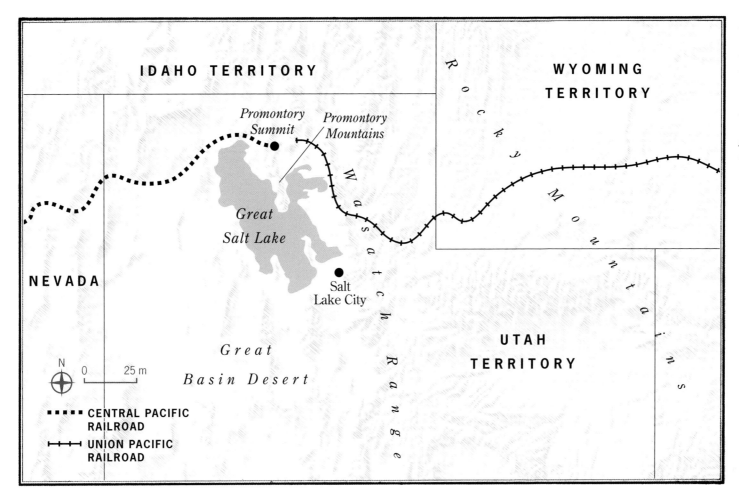

IDAHO TERRITORY

Promontory Summit

Promontory Mountains

WYOMING TERRITORY

Rocky Mountains

Great Salt Lake

NEVADA

Wasatch Range

Salt Lake City

Great Basin Desert

UTAH TERRITORY

N
0   25 m

▪▪▪▪ CENTRAL PACIFIC RAILROAD

┝┿┿┥ UNION PACIFIC RAILROAD

By the end of the first week of May 1869, what had seemed impossible not long before was on the verge of taking place. The tracks of the Central Pacific and those of the Union Pacific stood face-to-face, waiting to be joined.

With the linking site now officially chosen, both sides, determined to be the first to reach that now coveted spot, stepped up the pace as never before. And soon the construction of the great road took on a whole new look. For more than six years, the two companies had labored hundreds of miles away from each other. Now, in the vast, barren Utah territory,

Central Pacific graders and tracklayers and their Union Pacific counterparts began to work within sight of one another. "Work is being vigorously prosecuted on the U.P.P.R. and C.P.P.R.," the *Deseret News* reported, "both lines running near each other and occasionally crossing. . . . The grading camps present the appearance of a mighty army. As far as the eye can reach [there is] almost a continuous line of tents, wagons and men."

The grading gangs from the two companies were in fact now working so close together that when one of the gangs set off a blasting charge to loosen frozen earth, flying chunks of soil rained down on the heads of the other company's workers. It was not long before things got out of hand. Angered when some of their companions were injured by heavy flying debris, the Union Pacific's laborers began throwing clods of frozen earth at the Central Pacific's workers. Then they went after them with pickaxes. Not content with that, they deliberately set off explosions that killed several CP men. Both terrified and outraged, the UP workforce responded by setting off explosions of their own. In the resulting blasts, a number of Union Pacific workmen were buried alive by dirt and rocks.

Alarmed that the rivalry between the two companies had turned to bloodshed, officials of the Union Pacific and Central Pacific stepped in and ordered the hostilities to stop. But bitter feelings between rival workmen would remain until the very last rails were laid.

No one looked forward to the final laying of the rails more than Jack Casement, Grenville Dodge, Charlie Crocker, and James Strobridge. But as far as Crocker and Strobridge were concerned, there was still one huge bit of business to be dealt with before the Central Pacific finished laying its tracks. Neither had ever gotten over the fact that the Union Pacific could lay claim to having set down about eight miles of rail in a single day. "They bragged of it," Crocker remembered, "and it was heralded all over the country as being the biggest day's track-laying that was ever known."

Crocker, in particular, was annoyed at the amount of attention the Union Pacific had received in the nation's newspapers for its eight-mile achievement. And he still had not gotten over the amount of positive press that Durant had garnered for the UP through his excursion to the 100th meridian. Crocker simply would not let the railroad be completed without the Central Pacific capturing more glory than its rival.

Crocker would have Strobridge and his army of workers set a new record by laying down an unheard-of ten miles of track in a single day. Not only that, but he would make this record impossible for the Union Pacific to beat by waiting to attempt it until the UP's tracks were less than ten miles from the designated spot for the linking of the rails at Promontory Summit. That way, Casement's crews would not have enough distance left to try to better the ten-mile feat.

Ten miles in one day? Almost no one who got wind of Crocker's intention gave it any chance of succeeding. That included Durant, who simply laughed at the idea. Angered by his rival's reaction, Crocker bet the Union Pacific leader the princely sum of ten thousand dollars that the Central Pacific would indeed lay ten miles of rail in a single day. Durant immediately accepted the wager.

The bet had been made in October 1868. Now, six months later on April 28, 1869, Crocker was ready to try to win it. He had waited, as he had planned, until the Union Pacific was less than ten miles from Promontory Summit. And he had spent as much time as he could spare planning the event. If an "impossible" ten miles of track were to be laid in just one day, every step of the operation would have to have been planned in advance; everything would have to go like clockwork; there could be no wasted effort.

When the first faint light of dawn appeared on the 28th, Crocker was more than ready to begin. So too were the more than one thousand Central Pacific workmen whom he had organized into teams, each with a specific task. Aside from the glory that was to be gained, each of the workers had been given another incentive. Winning the bet and gaining the publicity it would engender had become so important to Crocker that he had thrown caution to the wind and promised the laborers that they would receive four times the wages they normally received for a working day.

That this was to be no ordinary working day was obvious to everyone present. Among the crowd that had gathered to view the much publicized event were Jack and Dan Casement and other Union Pacific officials, delighted to be on hand to witness what they were certain would be a colossal failure. Their opinion was shared by many of the newsmen who were also part of the growing throng.

Suddenly, the air was pierced by the shrill blast of a locomotive whistle. The attempt was on. Even before the whistle had sounded, crews of Chinese laborers had gathered beside dozens of open railroad freight cars loaded with rails, spikes, bolts, and other tracklaying materials. Before the sound of the whistle had died, they had begun loading enough of these items for two miles of track onto sixteen horse-drawn handcars that they delivered at breakneck speed to crews waiting to lay the tracks. By the time they arrived, workers called pioneers had straightened out the ties that had been laid on the ground the night before. As soon as the rails were unloaded, eight Irish workmen lifted them onto the ties. There was good reason why these tracklayers had been specially selected. Each of the rails they hefted was thirty feet long and weighed 560 pounds.

A steady stream of wagons hauling railroad ties makes its way to the head of the tracklaying action.

The sound of the rails being dropped onto the ties was still reverberating when gaugers quickly stepped forward to make sure that they were the correct distance apart. Within seconds, spikers began attaching rails to the ties. As the spikers made their way down each section of track, tampers followed immediately behind them, hammering down any spike that had not been securely fastened. All the while, the Chinese workers continued racing back and forth between supply trains and the advancing tracks.

"The scene is a most animated one," wrote one newsman. "From the first pioneer to the last tamper, perhaps two miles, there is a thin line of 1,000 men advancing a mile an hour . . . mounted men galloping backward and forward. Alongside of the moving force are teams hauling tools."

The reporters were not the only ones who were impressed. As Crocker surveyed the scene, his arm was suddenly grabbed by an excited high-ranking army officer who had come to witness the event. "I never saw such organization as this," the military man exclaimed, "it is just like an army marching across over the ground and leaving a track built behind them."

At 1:30 p.m., the locomotive whistle that had signaled the beginning of the day sounded again. It was time for lunch. The thousand-man "army" had worked nonstop for six hours. And they had laid six miles of track. As soon as the lunch break began, Strobridge approached the eight rail setters who had set down every rail over the entire six miles. Their work was done, he told them. They had to be exhausted, and he had another eight-man crew ready to relieve them. But they would have none of it. No one was going to replace them. They would see the job through to the finish.

And they did. After lunch the resumption of tracklaying was delayed almost an hour while workers hammered and bent the rails to fit the curves of a slope of the Promontory Mountains that lay ahead. It did not deter Crocker or Strobridge or their men, who, with their goal in sight, were more determined than ever to reach it. They worked for the next four and a half hours at the same incredible pace with which they had started the day. At 7:00 p.m., the locomotive whistle sounded once again. A precise measurement had just been taken. Ten miles and fifty-six feet of track had been laid.

Still, Crocker and Strobridge were not satisfied. They did not want to give the Union Pacific officials or the members of the press who were on hand the opportunity to question whether, in their determination, the laborers had done less than a perfect job. After the historic mark had been achieved, Strobridge, to prove that the grading and tracklaying had indeed been carried out exactly as they should have been, had almost all the men who had accomplished the extraordinary feat pile onto a long line of railroad cars whose two heavy engines backed smoothly down the rails at a rapid clip.

"We backed down over that sixty-six foot of grade at the rate of twenty-five miles an hour," Strobridge later wrote, "twelve hundred men riding on the empty flat cars. Two Union Pacific engineers were there with their surveying [instruments], so there was no guess work."

It was an astonishing accomplishment. In a single day, the Central Pacific's crew had positioned 25,800 ties, had laid 3,520 rails, had hammered 28,160 spikes, and had turned 14,080 bolts. In the process, they had laid an astonishing 240 feet of track every minute. Even more amazing, perhaps, were the accomplishments of the eight tracklayers. Together they had lifted and put into place 2,112,000 pounds of iron. That was 264,000 pounds each—all in one day!

In 1917, Strobridge granted author Lardin Fulton a series of interviews for a book Fulton was writing titled *Epic of the Overland.* In one of the

James Strobridge (center foreground, in suit) poses at what he named Camp Victory after the Central Pacific completed its historic feat of laying ten miles of track in a single day. Flush with success, Strobridge declared that if the Union Pacific had never existed, the Central Pacific could have laid the 1,086 miles of track from Promontory Summit to Omaha in less than eighteen months.

interviews that made its way into the book, Strobridge made certain that he named the eight tracklayers. It was an important acknowledgment. Among the hundreds of accounts that were written as the rails were laid across the continent, this was one of only a few times in which a group of workers was cited by name.

"H. H. Minkler was the foreman laying rails," Strobridge recounted, "and the men who handled them were Mike Shay, Mike Kennedy, Mike Sullivan, Pat Joyce, Tom Daily, George Wyatt, E. W. Killeen and Fred McNamara. . . . Nobody was crowded, nobody was hurt, nobody lost a minute."

When it was finally over, Jack Casement sought out James Strobridge and congratulated him for having accomplished what he had been certain could not be done. Dan Casement, however, was not as gracious. Devastated by the Central Pacific's victory and convinced that his Union Pacific could better that mark if they had enough miles to do so, he pleaded with Durant to let him go back and tear up several miles of track so they could prove it. But Durant turned him down. After which, as far as anyone knows, Durant acted in his typical manner. He never paid Crocker the ten thousand dollars he owed him for having lost the bet.

9

CELEBRATION

The Central Pacific's extraordinary achievement had done more than give it the glory that Crocker and Strobridge sought. When the historic ten-mile day was over, the company's tracks stood within just a few miles of Promontory Summit. "The last blow has been struck on the Central Pacific Railroad, and the last tie and rail were placed in position today," the *Alta California* proclaimed on April 30. "We are now waiting for the Union Pacific to finish their rock-cutting."

Only about eight miles from the linking spot, the Union Pacific's workers were being forced to blast their way through the stubborn rocks of the Promontory range that bordered Promontory Summit. Frustrated by having encountered this one last hurdle so close to the finish, Casement called on his men to make a final all-out effort. "Between six and seven hundred graders and one hundred track-layers are working . . . and now only twenty-five feet of rock-cutting remains to be finished," the *Alta California* reported. "Work will be carried on all night, and by tomorrow noon the grading will be entirely completed."

Union Pacific graders prepare a roadbed in the foothills of the Promontory Mountains.

As the newspaper predicted, the difficult grading was indeed completed, the final tracks were laid, and one week after the Central Pacific's rails had reached Promontory Summit, the Union Pacific's tracks stood opposite them with only a 2,500-foot gap between. The most captivating race in the nation's history was over. Ironically, neither company could legitimately claim itself the winner. While the Central Pacific was the first to reach the linking site, the Union Pacific had laid the greatest number of miles of track. And, despite all the obstacles that both had been forced to overcome and the incredible distance each had traveled, their final tracks had reached the immediate vicinity of Promontory Summit at about the same time.

The stage was set for the linking of the rails. It was also set for the releasing of most of the men who had performed a construction miracle. On May 1, hundreds of CP and UP workers lined up at their companies' paymasters' cars and were given their final wages. Thousands more were told that they would be required to work only one week more. "The two opposing armies . . . are melting away," the *Alta California* declared, and "the white camps which dotted every brown hillside and every shady glen . . . are being broken up and abandoned. The Central Pacific force are nearly all gone already, and that of the Union is going fast."

An elaborate ceremony featuring the official joining of the tracks had been scheduled for May 8, 1869. The Central Pacific's president, Leland Stanford, arrived for the festivities that morning, but not in his accustomed style. He had planned to make a grand entrance in the Central Pacific's fanciest and most luxurious train. But en route, an enormous tree trunk had come crashing down on the train, and Stanford and his large party of Central Pacific officials and guests were forced to abandon it for a much less distinguished train that had been hastily summoned.

Once he arrived at Promontory Summit, Stanford got another surprise. As soon as he stepped off the substitute train, Jack Casement informed him that the ceremonies scheduled for that day had been postponed until May 10. The train carrying Tom Durant and other Union Pacific officials and their guests had been delayed by a washed-out bridge.

Even though the bridge collapse had caused a delay, it was not the main reason Durant held up the ceremonies. On May 6, after the washout problem had been solved, Durant had faced a far greater trauma. As his train was entering Piedmont, Wyoming, it was suddenly halted by an armed mob of angry Union Pacific workers. The men then switched Durant's private car to a side track and chained it to a rail. Boarding the car, they took Durant captive at gunpoint, telling him that he would not be released until he paid them the large sum of money he owed them in back wages. Durant had no choice but to telegraph UP headquarters for the money. Only after it arrived and he turned it over to the disgruntled workers was he allowed to resume his journey and hastily make his way to the linking ceremony.

For a spot that would be the site of one of the greatest moments in the history of the nation, Promontory Summit was a horrible place. Aside from its desolate location, it had only one street, and most of its inhabitants lived not in houses but tents. It did, however, have saloons, which had led to rowdiness not unlike that which had taken place in the Hell on Wheels towns. According to newspaper reports, twenty-four men were murdered in the whiskey-filled town in the twenty-five days before the two railroads arrived.

But all that was forgotten as May 10, 1869, dawned bright and beautiful. By seven in the morning, the first spectators for the event that would change America had begun gathering at the spot where the rails would be joined. An hour later, a UP construction train carrying graders and tracklayers, who had delayed their leave-taking so that they could witness the great event, arrived. Shortly after ten o'clock, Durant's train, also carrying

The old and the new. The train carrying Leland Stanford to the linking ceremonies passes would-be settlers moving west by covered wagon, a method of transportation soon to be made obsolete by the train.

Grenville Dodge and Jack and Dan Casement, made its appearance. Along with these men there was a battalion from the 21st Infantry Regiment and two different military bands.

When all these latest arrivals had taken their places among the spectators, a group of the CP's Chinese workmen carefully graded the remaining section of land between the tracks of the two rival companies. Then they laid down the last ties and rails and drove in all but the final spikes. It was an extraordinary moment. "We stood with mouths agape," J. W. Malloy, one of the soldiers in the throng, recalled, "as we realized that the much talked-of line was completed."

Grenville Dodge was equally struck by the moment and all that the Union Pacific had achieved, particularly in the last year's push toward the linking site. "From the first day of April, 1868, until May 10, 1869, only thirteen months," he later wrote, "we built and laid . . . 555 miles of [track] and graded the line to Humboldt Wells, making the total distance covered by our force 726 miles, and transported all the materials and supplies from the Missouri River. When you consider that not a mile of this division of the road had been [surveyed] until April, that we covered in that year over 700 miles of road, bringing all the material from the Missouri River, that we had to overcome its two great physical obstacles, two ranges of mountains, it was a task never equalled then nor surpassed since."

With the two engines standing nose to nose, the formal ceremonies began. There were many speeches, all of them mercifully short, and several lively renditions of patriotic songs by the military bands. But the main event was the driving in of the railroad's final spike, a dramatic symbol that the great iron road had been completed. It was no ordinary spike, but one especially created for the celebration. To fit the occasion, it was made of gold.

Spectators from the Union Pacific and Central Pacific construction crews wait for the linking of the rails to begin.

"This spike," the *Alta California* informed its readers, "weighs about eighteen ounces and is valued at $350 [about $5,000 today]. A nugget about six inches in length is attached to the head of the spike, and will be broken off at the conclusion of the ceremonies to be made up into mementos." The following is the inscription:

THE PACIFIC RAILROAD GROUND BROKEN
JANY 8TH, 1863 AND COMPLETED MAY 8TH, 1869
MAY GOD CONTINUE THE UNITY OF OUR COUNTRY AS THIS
RAILROAD UNITES THE TWO GREAT OCEANS OF THE WORLD.

The driving of the Golden Spike has been continuously celebrated as one of the greatest moments in the nation's history. The spike, today regarded as a national treasure, was designed by jeweler David Hewes and manufactured by the San Francisco firm of Schulz, Fischer & Mahling. "There was one last thing to be done," Hewes would later write. "As an individual, I presented a gold spike and polished laurel tie with a silver shield on which was inscribed as follows: 'The last tie which unites in part, and helps complete the great road across the Continent.'" After the ceremony at Promontory Summit, the Golden Spike was removed so that it wouldn't be stolen or damaged.

Everyone present was well aware that this uniting of "the two great oceans of the world" had, in no small measure, been made possible by the rivalry of the great race. So no one should really have been surprised that it continued to the very last act of the adventure. The question of the hour was: Who was to have the honor of driving in this final spike? Governor Stanford insisted that he should be the one. Tom Durant declared that he deserved to do it. The argument continued until just five minutes before the spike was driven. Finally, Durant gave in and reluctantly handed the honor over to Stanford.

For such an extraordinarily important event, the crowd at the joining of the rails was relatively small. But, thanks to the telegraph, word that East and West had been linked was quickly relayed to a waiting nation.

PRESERVING THE ADVENTURE

AS THE TRANSCONTINENTAL RAILROAD was being built, the Central Pacific's and the Union Pacific's graders, tracklayers, and tens of thousands of other workers were not the only ones making a steady march across the continent. The entire adventure was preserved by photographers who recorded almost every aspect of what eventually would be called a construction miracle.

One of these cameramen, Andrew J. Russell, was hired by the Union Pacific to be its official photographer. During the Civil War, he took scores of pictures of military railroad construction. It was an experience that prepared him well for what he accomplished with the Union Pacific. Russell's Central Pacific counterpart was Alfred A. Hart. He began his career as a portrait painter. But once he was hired by the CP to be its official photographer, he dedicated himself to overcoming the immense challenges of capturing images in steep mountain terrain and scorching deserts.

Photographer's wagons, such as this one, were a common sight along the entire route of the transcontinental railroad. The cloth-draped box served as a portable developing room.

There were dozens of other photographers who, either on their own or in the employ of a newspaper, magazine, or photographic company, recorded the laying of the rails across the continent. Among them were Alexander Gardner, arguably the most talented of all the Civil War photographers, and Charles R. Savage, known for his early landscape views of the American West.

Following the tracks through some of the most difficult and dangerous terrain imaginable, living out in the open in extraordinary extremes of weather, the photographers experienced many of the same challenges the railroad laborers were forced to endure. And, like the workmen, they had to operate with equipment much different from that of today.

The cameras of the 1860s were large, heavy, and cumbersome. The invention of photographic film was still more than twenty years away. The photographs were captured on fragile large glass plates. On more than one occasion, after one of the photographers had spent an entire day photographing in the mountains or in other difficult landscapes, the mule carrying his image-bearing plates slipped, the plates fell to the ground and shattered, and all of the photographer's work was destroyed.

Still, like the laborers whose accomplishments they captured, the photographers would not allow themselves to be discouraged. As a result, they left us an exceptional permanent record of one of the nation's greatest achievements.

By capturing spectacular images such as this one, photographers compiled an invaluable record of one of America's greatest adventures. The cameraman standing next to his wagon at the bottom of the picture is Andrew J. Russell, the Union Pacific's official photographer.

No one expected Stanford to be able to pound the spike in very far. A hole had been dug where the spike was to be inserted so that it could go in at least a little way. But no one expected him to miss the spike completely. Yet, to the great amusement of the crowd, he did. Among the spectators amused was Alexander Toponce. A true American pioneer and mountain man, Toponce had been a cowboy, a stagecoach driver, a Pony Express rider, and a gold prospector. Later, in his autobiography, he described what happened when Stanford missed the spike. "What a howl went up!" he wrote. "Irish, Chinese, Mexicans and everybody yelled with delight, 'He missed it! Yee!'"

Fully embarrassed, Stanford turned the sledgehammer over to Durant. And he also missed it. "Everybody slapped everybody else again and yelled, 'he missed it too,'" Toponce wrote.

The sledge that Stanford and Durant had wielded was no ordinary hammer. Attached to it was a wire that led to a telegraph key operated by a man seated at a table close to the action. Of all those at the festivities, he was the most important. The entire nation was anxiously waiting for the news that the last spike had been driven, that East and West had been joined. In cities throughout the country, other telegraph operators were standing by, ready to receive the historic news, ready to relay it to the waiting crowds. As Stanford prepared to step forward, the operator at Promontory sent his first message: "TO EVERYBODY, KEEP QUIET. WHEN THE LAST SPIKE IS DRIVEN AT PROMONTORY POINT, WE WILL SAY 'DONE!' DON'T BREAK THE CIRCUIT, BUT WATCH FOR THE SIGNALS OF THE BLOWS OF THE HAMMER." As Stanford took up the hammer, the operator sent a second message: "ALMOST READY. HATS OFF; PRAYER IS BEING OFFERED." Less than two minutes later, the wires came alive again. "WE HAVE GOT DONE PRAYING. THE SPIKE IS ABOUT TO BE PRESENTED."

The wired hammer that Stanford had swung struck the iron rail instead of the spike, but the rail was actually an even better conductor of electricity than the spike. Immediately, the telegraph operator relayed the magic word: "DONE!"

When the last of the ceremonial spikes were driven, the Central Pacific's locomotive Jupiter *and the Union Pacific's locomotive No. 109 were brought face-to-face. The picture that Andrew J. Russell took of the Central Pacific's chief engineer, Samuel Montague (left), and the Union Pacific's chief engineer, Grenville Dodge (right), waving wine bottles in celebration has become one of the most famous photographs ever taken.*

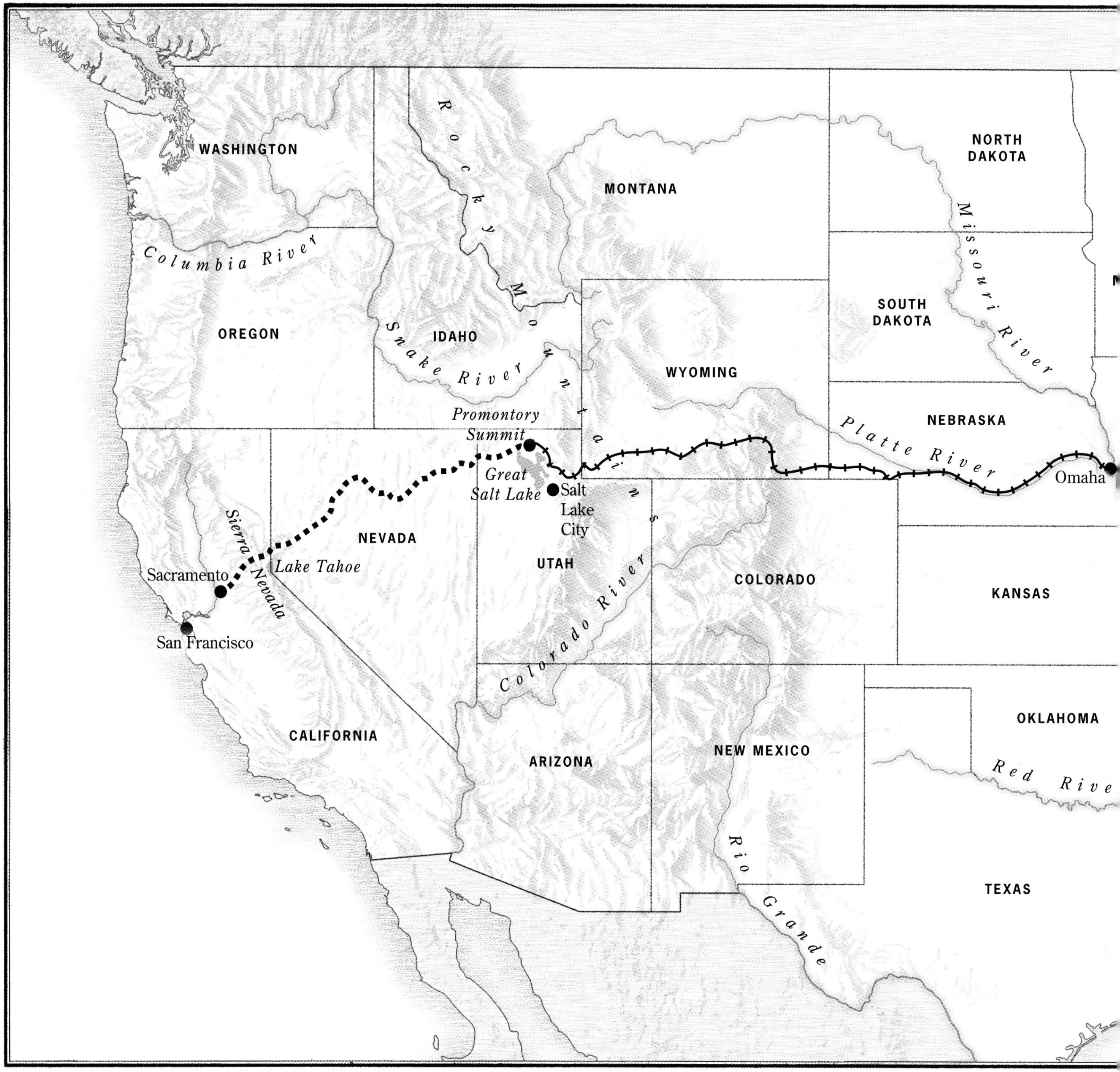

The routes of the Central
Pacific and Union Pacific
railroads as of 1869,
shown on a map of the
present-day United Sates.

WASHINGTON

NORTH
DAKOTA

MONTANA

Columbia River

OREGON

Snake River

IDAHO

Rocky Mountains

SOUTH
DAKOTA

Missouri River

WYOMING

NEBRASKA

Platte River

Promontory
Summit

Omaha

_Great
Salt Lake_

Salt
Lake
City

Sierra Nevada

NEVADA

UTAH

Colorado River

COLORADO

Sacramento

Lake Tahoe

KANSAS

San Francisco

OKLAHOMA

CALIFORNIA

ARIZONA

NEW MEXICO

Red River

Rio Grande

TEXAS

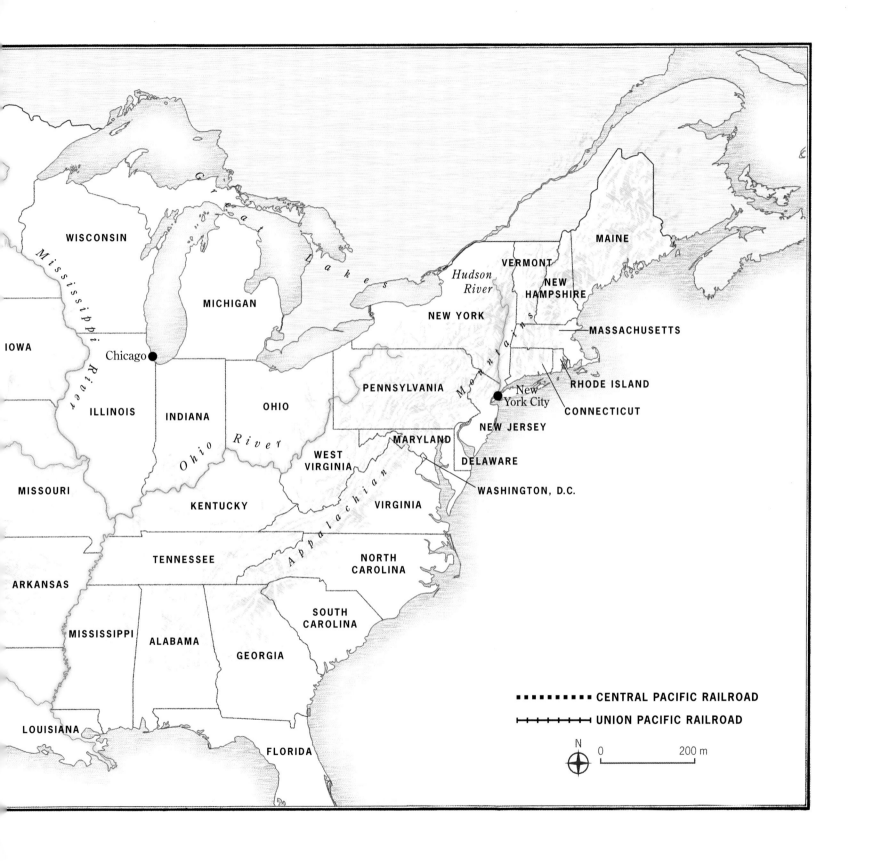

WISCONSIN

MICHIGAN

Mississippi River

IOWA

Chicago

ILLINOIS

INDIANA

OHIO

MISSOURI

KENTUCKY

Ohio River

Great Lakes

Hudson River

VERMONT

NEW HAMPSHIRE

MAINE

NEW YORK

MASSACHUSETTS

PENNSYLVANIA

Mountains

RHODE ISLAND

New York City

CONNECTICUT

NEW JERSEY

MARYLAND

DELAWARE

WEST VIRGINIA

WASHINGTON, D.C.

VIRGINIA

Appalachian

TENNESSEE

NORTH CAROLINA

ARKANSAS

SOUTH CAROLINA

MISSISSIPPI

ALABAMA

GEORGIA

LOUISIANA

FLORIDA

·········· CENTRAL PACIFIC RAILROAD

├┼┼┼┼┼┤ UNION PACIFIC RAILROAD

N

0   200 m

With this single word, the country exploded into one of the greatest celebrations it had ever had. In every city and town, church bells, fireworks, and fire alarms went off and lasted well into the night. Factory whistles sounded throughout the nation. In Philadelphia, the Liberty Bell rang. In Washington, a ball atop a pole set high above the Capitol building was dropped while thousands of people roared with delight. In New York, a two-hundred-gun salute split the air. Omaha fired its own hundred-cannon salvo. In Sacramento, thirty decorated locomotives, drawn up in a line, blew their whistles.

No place in America was without its celebration. San Franciscans danced in the streets. People in Buffalo gathered together to sing "The Star-Spangled Banner." The citizens of Chicago staged a spontaneous parade that stretched for seven miles. In Salt Lake City, Mormons knelt down in prayer.

Back at Promontory Summit, the festivities were not quite over. James Strobridge, Grenville Dodge, Jack Casement, and other officials from both the Central Pacific and the Union Pacific were given the honor of striking ceremonial spikes. The honor of being the last to hit a spike was given to Hanna Strobridge, in recognition of her being the only woman to have been present throughout the building of the road.

One woman, however, was completely overlooked. No one had thought of inviting Theodore Judah's widow, Anna, who had so earnestly encouraged her husband and who had actually accompanied him on several of his forays into the Sierras that had made the whole enterprise possible. Back in Greenfield, Massachusetts, Anna Judah was well aware of what was taking place clear across the continent. "The spirit of my brave husband," she would later write, "descended upon me, and together we were there unseen."

When all the celebrations were over, and the cheering had died down, there was time to reflect on what had been accomplished. General William Sherman, for whom Sherman Summit had been named, was unable to attend the linking ceremonies, but like Anna Judah, he had been there in spirit. The day after the final rails were laid, he wrote to his old friend and former military colleague Grenville Dodge. "In common with millions," Sherman wrote, "I sat yesterday and heard the mystic taps of the telegraph battery announce the nailing of the last spike in the great Pacific road. . . . All honor to you . . . and the thousands of brave fellows who have wrought out this glorious problem, spite of changes, storms, and even doubts of the incredulous, and all the obstacles you have now happily surmounted."

Many of the tributes were written by those who had been present at the final spiking. Captain J. E. Currier and his wife traveled from New Hampshire to be at the linking of the rails. "We have just witnessed the laying of the last rail," he wrote. "Truly it is worth a trip from New Hampshire to see this alone. . . . Nattie and myself were permitted to give a stroke upon the hammer. I drove my spike with my sword hilt. . . . Thus is the greatest undertaking of the 19th century accomplished. All honors to the resolute men who have 'put it through.'"

Perhaps the most prophetic statement of all was made by a Union Pacific surveyor who was in attendance. "'Tis Finished!" he wrote. "This great and mighty enterprise that spans a continent with iron and unites two oceans . . . the future is coming and fast too."

It was not just coming. It had arrived, and it would bring with it the greatest changes in the shortest period of time that any nation had ever experienced. There was no mystery about what would cause these transformations. As future president James A. Garfield would eventually state, "The changes now taking place have been wrought and are being wrought mainly, almost wholly, by a single mechanical contrivance, the steam loco-motive. The railway is the greatest centralizing force of modern times." He meant the transcontinental.

The first and most obvious change was in the extraordinarily reduced time it took to cross the country. On May 15, 1869, the transcontinental railroad began regular passenger service. Once a day, westbound pas-sengers boarded the Pacific Express in Omaha and began the journey to Sacramento. And once a day in Sacramento, eastbound travelers climbed

For hundreds of years the vast territory between the Mississippi and the Rocky Mountains had been referred to as the Great American Desert. This artist's depiction shows the region that came to be known as the Great West.

aboard the Atlantic Express and began their almost two-thousand-mile trip to Omaha, with connecting service to New York. The cross-country trip that for so long had taken six months was now reduced to less than a week. "A journey over the plains was [formerly] a formidable undertaking, that required great patience and endurance," exclaimed *Frank Leslie's Illustrated Newspaper*. "Now all is changed. The shriek of the locomotive wakes the echoes of the slopes of the Sierras, through the [canyons] of the Wasatch and the Black Hills, and his steady puffing is heard as he creeps along the mountain sides. . . . The prairie schooner has passed away, and is replaced by the railway coach with all its modern comforts."

Even the staunchest supporters of the transcontinental had underestimated the immediate sensation the railway would become. "Every man [and woman] who could command the time and money was eager to make the trip," one reporter declared. He was right. In 1870, the first full year of operations, some 150,000 passengers rode the line between Omaha and Sacramento.

Whether they arrived in Sacramento after traveling westward, or in New York or Boston after traveling eastward and changing trains in Omaha, America's first cross-country railroad passengers experienced even more than an unprecedented railroad journey. Thanks to the transcontinental, they witnessed a new United States in the making. "After crossing the vastness of the American West, the endless unclaimed fertile lands, the prairies and forests, the broad rivers and towering mountains," historian Dee Brown wrote, "[the passengers] felt that they had seen a new map unrolled, a new empire revealed, a new civilization in the process of creation." "I felt patriotically proud," one Sacramento arrival would write. "[The nation had been bound] by links of iron that can never be broken."

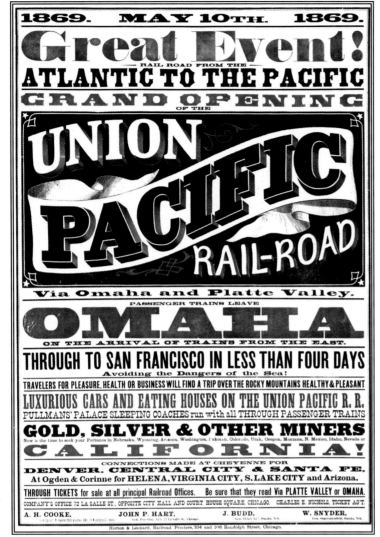

By the time the transcontinental railroad was completed, posters had become an effective means of advertising. Officials of both the Union Pacific and the Central Pacific used posters like this one to attract passengers to the newly opened cross-country line.

It was not only people moving about with unprecedented speed thanks to the transcontinental. Dramatic transformation took place in the shipment of goods and mail as well. Manufacturers and merchants who, until the linking of the rails, had to rely on ox-drawn or horse-drawn wagons or on sailing vessels or steamboats to move their products could now ship them across country in days at a fraction of their previous cost. The same great transformation affected the delivery of mail from one coast to the other. Placed aboard the transcontinental, mail that had previously cost several dollars per ounce and had taken months to be delivered now could be shipped for pennies and be delivered in just a few days. By 1880, more than $50 million worth of goods and hundreds of thousands of letters and packages were being shipped across the continent over the great iron road.

The presence of the great road changed the very profile of the nation and was instrumental in the development of what became known as the Great

A TERRIBLE INJUSTICE

WHEN THE TRANSCONTINENTAL RAILROAD was completed, many of the Chinese former railroad workers settled in a section of Los Angeles that became known as Chinatown. Some found work in laundries or canneries; others became gardeners; still others took up farming. But no matter how hard they worked, they could not avoid the prejudice and discrimination that continued to plague them. Nor could they halt the emergence of politically powerful groups whose goal was to prevent any more Chinese people from entering the United States. Among those who spoke out for halting Chinese immigration was Leland Stanford. When he was president of the Central Pacific and needed Chinese labor, he had asked Congress to let as many Chinese workers into the country as possible. Now that he didn't need them anymore, he campaigned to keep them out.

On May 6, 1882, Stanford and those who felt as he did got their wish. Congress passed a law prohibiting all Chinese workers from entering the United States for the next ten years. It was called the Chinese Exclusion Act of 1882, and it was the first federal law ever passed in the United States banning a particular group from immigrating to America. The act had another provision. It prohibited all Chinese men and women who might otherwise have been granted U.S. citizenship from receiving it. Among those who were denied were many of the men who had built the transcontinental railroad.

In spite of all the obstacles, between 1910 and 1940 some 175,000 Chinese immigrants managed to enter the United States. Then, in 1941, World War II erupted. Japan's brutal invasion of China led to great public sympathy for Chinese Americans. Also, more than 13,000 Chinese-American soldiers served in the U.S. army with distinction, and Chinese laborers were needed in America's war industries. All these factors combined to bring about the repeal, in 1943, of the Chinese Exclusion Acts. Following the war, Chinese people began coming to the United States in record numbers. Today, the diverse ranks of the U.S. population include more than four million Chinese Americans.

West. The seemingly endless American prairie had been so sparsely settled that it was called the Great American Desert. But as those who followed the building of the transcontinental across the Great Plains quickly learned, the prairie soil was among the richest in the world. "The soil," a reporter from the *Cincinnati Gazette* wrote, "is very rich, and the mind falters in its attempt to estimate the future of such a valley, or its immense capacities. . . . The grain fields of Europe are mere garden patches beside the green oceans which roll across the Great Plains." Millions of immigrants, most of them farmers, traveled the transcontinental and poured into the West. By 1880, these newcomers had covered more than two million acres of land with crops and turned the American prairie into the breadbasket of the world.

The transcontinental railroad also facilitated as never before the way ideas and information could be quickly and continually exchanged between different regions of the vast nation. Thanks to the transcontinental, the nation, as it entered the twentieth century, became more unified in thought as well as deed than it had ever been before.

Sadly, not everyone benefited. That included both the Chinese workers who made up more than 80 percent of the Central Pacific's workforce and the American Indians. The building of the transcontinental railroad was far from the first occasion for battles between European-American immigrants and the Native Americans. And it was not the final series of happenings in these battles. But it was the greatest of all indicators of the encroachment of white society upon the Indians, an unstoppable encroachment that would eventually see those who had been first in America lose their land and their way of life and be forced onto reservations.

One of the arguments made in support of building the transcontinental railroad involved the prospect of opening up Asian trade to American merchants. Goods could be shipped to West Coast ports by rail. Many of those who had invested in the iron road had done so with this prospect in mind. But only six months after the rails were joined at Promontory Summit, another great construction project was completed. The Suez Canal, a man-made waterway that linked Europe with Asia, became known as the "Highway to India." The then 102-mile canal gave European merchants an advantage in the Asian trade that American merchants would not be able to overcome.

For American merchants, it was a huge disappointment. But it was greatly outweighed by the advantages the transcontinental brought the nation. Advantages so great and so obvious that by 1893, four more cross-country railroads had been constructed and dozens of smaller lines branched out from these main arteries.

The extraordinary achievement had started as what seemed an impossible dream. It had been made possible by men of incredible courage and determination. After the last of those who had laid the rails from Sacramento and Omaha had returned home, after the last spectators had left Promontory Summit, after the first transcontinental trains began to make their runs, there were many reflections on all that had been overcome in building the great road and all that had been accomplished. Among those who expressed them was the Union Pacific's Grenville Dodge. He spoke for his own company, but his words rang true for the Central Pacific as well.

"When you look back to the beginning at the Missouri River," Dodge wrote, "with no railway communication from the east and 500 miles of the country in advance without timber, fuel or any material whatever from which to build or maintain a road, except the sand for the bare roadbed itself; with everything to be created . . . you can all look back upon the work with satisfaction and ask, 'under such circumstances could we have done more or better?'"

EPILOGUE:
WHAT HAPPENED TO THEM

JACK CASEMENT

When his work on the transcontinental was completed, Jack Casement returned home to Painesville, Ohio. Hailed as a hero, he was elected to the Ohio Senate. But the man who had led troops in pitched battles in the Civil War and had led the Union Pacific halfway across the continent found life in a legislative chamber much too tame. By the late 1870s, accompanied by his brother Dan, he was off traveling again, and supervising the construction of various railroads in Canada and the United States.

For the next twenty years, Casement continued to move from one railroad project to another, and in 1897, nearing the age of seventy, he took on the job of overseeing the construction of a railroad through the jungles and mountains of Costa Rica. It was a challenge that in many ways was no less daunting than the building of the transcontinental had been. By this time, Dan had died, and Casement was joined in Costa Rica by one of his sons. For the better part of six years, the two Casements struggled to bring the road to completion. But in 1903, after outbreaks of yellow fever, mud slides, and other disasters had taken a horrific toll on his workers, Casement, for the first time in his life, was forced to abandon a project.

Still, his adventures were not over. In 1906, after completing yet another railroad endeavor, he was in a hotel on the outskirts of San Francisco when the devastating San Francisco earthquake struck. Buried in the debris when the hotel collapsed, he suffered serious injuries. Yet within a year he was back at it, always on the lookout for the next railroad to build.

The seemingly indestructible Casement was still working in 1909 when he developed pneumonia. The man who had led battalions of soldiers and armies of railroad workers died on December 13, 1909.

LEWIS CLEMENT

Lewis Clement, whose engineering genius made it possible for the Central Pacific to conquer Cape Horn and to construct the Summit Tunnel, would continue a life of considerable achievement once the transcontinental was completed. Shortly after his work on the great iron road was done, he joined the Southern Pacific Railroad Company and helped design and build its railroad from Sacramento to Los Angeles. When that project was completed, he was appointed chief engineer of the Western Division of the Atlantic and Pacific Railroad, which became part of the Santa Fe Railroad.

Clement was an accomplished inventor as well as an engineer. Among his inventions was the famous "Emigrant Sleeping Car," the railroad car that transported millions of settlers to the West once the transcontinentals were built. Clement also invented a machine that made it easier for railroad builders to bend rails to precise specifications. In 1881, Clement turned his attention to developing new methods of travel within cities. He became one of the nation's leading designers and builders of both cable and electric railway systems.

A highly cultured man, Clement was invited into many learned societies both in the United States and abroad. By the time he died, on October 29, 1914, at his home in Hayward, California, the many awards he received from these organizations made him arguably the most honored of all those who built the transcontinental railroad.

CHARLES CROCKER

When the transcontinental railroad was completed, Charlie Crocker, who had physically overseen the Central Pacific's arduous construction activities from the laying of its first rails to the last, was exhausted. Deciding to retire, he asked his fellow CP stockholders to buy him out. When they were ready to do so in 1873, a serious economic depression hit the United States and their payment to him was delayed. Meantime, Crocker, who had become bored in retirement, found new employment overseeing the construction of several railway lines that eventually became part of the Southern Pacific Railroad.

When Crocker was finally paid for his Central Pacific stock, he became an immensely wealthy man. He plunged into several new activities, including real estate development. His most important post-transcontinental undertaking was the establishment of a giant irrigation company, an operation that helped establish California as one of the leading agricultural states in the nation. In 1886, while on a visit to New York, Crocker was thrown from a carriage in which he was riding and seriously injured. He never fully recovered and died two years later in Monterey, California.

GRENVILLE DODGE

When Tom Durant held his excursion to celebrate the Union Pacific's having reached the 100th meridian, Grenville Dodge took part in the festivities and helped Durant stage many of the extravagant events. While he was doing so, and with no campaigning on his part, Dodge was elected to the U.S. Congress from his Iowa home district. He was so busy building the transcontinental, however, that he devoted almost no time to that position.

In 1872, when the Crédit Mobilier scandal became public knowledge, it was revealed that Dodge had made a great deal of money by secretly purchasing shares in Crédit Mobilier in his wife's name. To escape testifying before congressional committees investigating the scandal, the much-traveled Dodge fled to Texas, where he went into hiding.

During the 1880s and 1890s, Dodge emerged from hiding, went back into railroading, and served as president or chief engineer of several railroad companies. He also spent a good deal of time in New York, where he had established several businesses.

Because of his exploration, travels, and railroad building in the West, Dodge is well remembered there. His home in Council Bluffs, Iowa, where he died in 1916, is a National Historic Landmark. Fort Dodge, in Kansas, an important army base in America's frontier days, is named for him. So too is a well-traveled bridge that spans the Missouri River.

THOMAS DURANT

Immediately following the linking of the rails at Promontory Summit, almost everyone connected with the transcontinental was regarded with reverence by the American public. That included Tom Durant, who, among other honors, was elected a fellow of the prestigious American Society of Civil Engineers.

There was one group, however, that did not hold Durant in such high regard. For a long time, Durant's fellow members of the Union Pacific's board of directors tried to oust him from the board. They were fed up with the financial shenanigans that had enriched him while, on more than one occasion, coming close to bankrupting the UP. But just as the movement to remove Durant was gaining momentum, he beat his fellow directors to the punch and abruptly resigned from the Union Pacific shortly after the rails were joined at Promontory Summit. Taking the millions he had made, particularly through the scandalous Crédit Mobilier he had created, he moved on and, as historian Edwin Rozwenc wrote, "set out to set up other corrupt businesses and to pursue other fields of plunder."

For the slippery Durant, it was a fortunate move. Up to this point, the public had been unaware of the illegal nature of the Crédit Mobilier, and the fact that some of the nation's most important political leaders had made large sums of money through its maneuverings. But then, in 1872, a major American newspaper broke the story, naming names and revealing how the Crédit Mobilier had bilked the public. It would become the biggest political scandal of the century. The nation's vice president, Schuyler Colfax; a number of members of Congress; and certain Union Pacific officials would fall into disgrace.

Because he had distanced himself from the UP, Durant escaped the scandal relatively unscathed. But he would finally pay the price for his many outrageous actions. The man who on one hand had played a major role in making the transcontinental a reality, and on the other had been perhaps the greatest scoundrel in the entire endeavor, would spend the last twelve years of his life fighting lawsuits from disgruntled partners and investors he had cheated. Durant died in Warren County, New York, on October 5, 1885.

COLLIS HUNTINGTON

Collis Huntington, the man who wielded the most power in the Central Pacific, remained in railroading for the rest of his life. By acquiring the majority of stock in a number of expanding railway lines and attaining directorships in others, Huntington came to control a transportation system that stretched from the Atlantic to the Pacific.

Of all those responsible for building the transcontinental, Huntington was arguably the most complex of all. In his running of the Central Pacific he was manipulative and often ruthless. And he never let regard for the law either stand in the way of benefiting the CP or interfere with his attainment of enormous wealth. Yet, late in life, he devoted himself to a cause that changed the lives of some of the nation's most disadvantaged citizens.

On his many travels to the South, Huntington came into contact with African Americans whose parents and grandparents had been slaves. Determined to help them rise out of poverty, he became a chief financial supporter of both Hampton Normal and Agricultural Institute and Tuskegee Institute. These two schools were devoted to teaching young African Americans the trades and skills necessary to help them build better lives for themselves and their families.

Huntington also indirectly left behind another important legacy. He had no children, but he willed much of his immense estate to his nephew Henry E. Huntington. For the rest of his life, the nephew used much of his inheritance to accumulate a magnificent library of rare books and celebrated paintings. When he died, these treasures became the foundation of the Huntington Library, Art Collections, and Botanical Gardens in San Marino, California, forever linking Collis Huntington's wealth with the public good.

LELAND STANFORD

In many ways, Leland Stanford's life was even more interesting after the transcontinental railroad was completed than it was during the time he served as president of the Central Pacific. He remained involved in railroading and eventually became president of the Southern Pacific.

Stanford's interests, however, expanded far beyond railroads. Among them was his ownership of a 55,000-acre farm that contained the largest vineyard in California. He also bought a 19,000-acre ranch where experiments with growing new varieties of wheat took place. His greatest love, however, was horse racing, and yet another large ranch that he owned was devoted to the breeding of racehorses.

In 1884, Stanford's life took a dramatic turn when his fifteen-year-old son died during a trip to Europe. As a memorial to the boy, the enormously wealthy Stanford established Stanford University in his son's honor. In 1885, Stanford, who had previously served as governor of California, reentered politics and was twice elected to the U.S. Senate. He died in Palo Alto, California, on June 21, 1893.

JAMES STROBRIDGE

One of the closest relationships that developed during the building of the transcontinental railroad was that between James Strobridge and Charles Crocker, the two men most responsible for the Central Pacific's successfully laying tracks through the rough landscape that many thought would be impossible to penetrate. Similar in both perseverance and fiery temperament, Strobridge and Crocker followed similar paths once their work on the iron road was done.

After the Golden Spike ceremony in 1869, Strobridge, like Crocker, went into retirement, settling with his wife, Hanna, and their six children on a farm near Hayward, California. But, like Crocker, he soon became dissatisfied with being idle. In 1877, the two men joined forces again when Crocker asked Strobridge to help him oversee the construction of what would become a large section of a second transcontinental line. When that work was completed, Strobridge became a construction boss on two other lines, one from Mojave to Needles, California, the other up the Sacramento River Canyon toward Oregon. Strobridge continued supervising railroad construction until 1889, when, at the age of sixty-two, he retired to his farm, this time for good.

TIMELINE

1845

Asa Whitney's proposal for a transcontinental railroad comes before Congress, but is rejected.

MARCH 1853

Congress authorizes Secretary of War Jefferson Davis to organize surveys to determine the best route westward for a transcontinental railroad.

JULY 1860

Theodore Judah discovers a route for the transcontinental railroad through the Donner Pass in the Sierra Nevada.

NOVEMBER 1860

Theodore Judah secures investors for a company that will be named the Central Pacific Railroad. The principal directors of the company will become known as the Big Four.

JULY 1, 1862

Abraham Lincoln signs the Pacific Railway Act, authorizing the Central Pacific to build a transcontinental railroad line east from Sacramento. The bill also establishes the Union Pacific Railroad, authorizing it to build a transcontinental railroad line west from the Missouri River.

JANUARY 8, 1863

Groundbreaking ceremonies for the Central Pacific are held in Sacramento, California.

October 26, 1863

The Central Pacific lays down its first tracks.

October 30, 1863

Thomas Durant gains control of the Union Pacific Railroad.

December 2, 1863

The Union Pacific breaks ground in Omaha, Nebraska.

January 1865

Chinese workers are hired by the Central Pacific.

April 14, 1865

President Abraham Lincoln, one of the greatest champions of a transcontinental railroad, is assassinated.

July 10, 1865

The Union Pacific lays its first rails in Omaha, Nebraska.

Late Summer 1865

The Central Pacific begins the task of hand-drilling a dozen tunnels through the Sierra Nevada.

February 1866

Durant hires Jack Casement as construction boss for the Union Pacific.

May 1866

Durant hires Grenville Dodge as chief engineer for the Union Pacific.

October 1866

Durant stages a lavish excursion to celebrate the Union Pacific reaching the 100th meridian.

Fort Kearny in the Nebraska Territory becomes the first Hell on Wheels town.

July 4, 1867

Grenville Dodge founds the town of Cheyenne in the Wyoming Territory.

August 7, 1867

A group of Cheyenne warriors stages a raid on Union Pacific tracks and a Union Pacific supply train at Plum Creek, Nebraska.

August 28, 1867

Central Pacific workers succeed in blasting through the rock of the Summit Tunnel.

December 13, 1867

Chinese workers for the Central Pacific set down the first rails across the Nevada line.

April 16, 1868

Union Pacific workers lay tracks through Sherman Summit in the Rocky Mountains, the highest point on the transcontinental railroad.

MAY 1868

Mormon laborers begin performing grading and blasting operations for both the Union Pacific and the Central Pacific in Utah.

JANUARY 1869

Corinne, Utah, becomes the last of the Hell on Wheels towns.

APRIL 9, 1869

Promontory Summit, Utah, is chosen as the site for the linking of the rails of the Central Pacific and the Union Pacific.

APRIL 28, 1869

One thousand UP workmen lay ten miles of track in one day.

MAY 6, 1869

Unpaid Union Pacific workers hold Durant hostage in his railroad car until he pays them the back wages that are due them.

MAY 10, 1869

The Golden Spike ceremonies, celebrating the linking of the Central Pacific's and the Union Pacific's tracks, are held at Promontory Summit, Utah.

MAY 15, 1869

The transcontinental railroad begins regular passenger service.

SOURCE NOTES

Page references in italics indicate caption text.

Key to abbreviations:

CPRPHM: Central Pacific Railroad Photographic History Museum

UPRM: Union Pacific Railroad Museum

Back cover: "It is a grand 'anvil chorus' . . . America is complete." *Fortnightly Review* 9,
p. 572. UPRM.

PROLOGUE

p. ix: "amusement, curiosity . . . profound respect." *Fortnightly Review* 9, p. 572. UPRM.

pp. ix–x: "On they came . . . America is complete." Ibid.

p. xi: "giants." CPRPHM.

p. xi: "These men . . . in railway history." UPRM.

CHAPTER 1: DREAMERS AND BUILDERS

p. 1: "shrink the continent . . . the whole world." CPRPHM.

p. 1: "It is in . . . shores firmly together." Bain, p. 17.

p. 2: "the greatest public . . . ever yet accomplished." *Skamania County Pioneer,* May 9, 1907.
CPRPHM.

p. 3: "create settlements, commerce and wealth." CPRPHM.

p. 3: "to unite neighboring . . . with each other." Rothstein.

p. 3: "a big blank slate." "The Transcontinental Railroad," *American Experience.*

pp. 3–4: "Any transcontinental railroad . . . a locomotive uphill." Kraus, p. 8.

p. 5: "to build . . . to the moon." Brown, p. 28.

p. 6: "What do we . . . cheerless and uninviting." Kraus, p. 13.

pp. 6–7: "A railroad, from . . . the United States." *Report on Railroads to the Senate of California,* January 1851. CPRPHM.

p. 7: "the necessity that . . . conceded by every one." House Select Committee on the Pacific Railroad and Telegraph Report, August 16, 1856. CPRPHM.

p. 7: "A railroad from . . . on the ground." *Putnam's Monthly Magazine,* November 1853. CPRPHM.

p. 7: "practical and economical." Brown, p. 34.

p. 8: "Not since Napoleon . . . under one banner." UPRM.

p. 10: "Anna, I am going . . . of the Pacific Coast." Williams, p. 30.

p. 13: "A railroad to . . . in its construction." Ambrose, p. 40.

p. 14: "We have drawn . . . harness him up." "The Transcontinental Railroad," *American Experience.*

p. 14: "Each [of us] . . . director of men." Kraus, p. 294.

p. 16: "I had all . . . along with them." "The Transcontinental Railroad," *American Experience.*

p. 17: "Wanted, 5,000 laborers . . . work, near Auburn." Ambrose, p. 148.

p. 17: "I will not boss Chinese." O'Connor, p. 74. CPRPHM.

p. 17: "They built the . . . a railroad." Brown, p. 74.

p. 18: "men generally earn . . . work for me." Ambrose, p. 164.

p. 18: "The truth is . . . suits Strobridge." CPRPHM.

p. 19: "would not discredit San Francisco." Ambrose, p. 314.

p. 19: "the heroine of the CP." Ibid.

p. 20: "The experiment . . . proved eminently successful." Williams, p. 97.

p. 23: "If you want . . . the last spike." Ambrose, p. 117.

CHAPTER 2: RAILS ACROSS THE PLAINS

p. 27: "made by the . . . California and Oregon." Dodge, p. 5.

p. 27: "I took a . . . [through these mountains]." Ibid., p. 20.

p. 28: "Mr. Lincoln sat . . . of my reconnaissances." Ibid., p. 11.

p. 28: "We don't know . . . he has been." UPRM.

p. 29: "greatest enterprise under God." Ibid.

p. 31: "They were strong . . . drink to them." Barter, p. 36.

p. 32: "The organization for . . . or any emergency." Dodge, p. 118.

pp. 34–35: "It is half . . . and steps across." Wheeler, p. 100.

pp. 35–36: "To supply one . . . to our transportation." UPRM.

p. 40: *Achan! Achan! Achan!* . . . tired of talking." Mayer and Vose, p. 98.

p. 40: "a grand and appalling sight." Ambrose, p. 141.

p. 41: "not only . . . but intelligently." Dodge, p. 111.

p. 44: "What unites them . . . coming on behind." Klein, p. 136.

p. 45: "[The crew chief] . . . its regulation beat." Ambrose, p. 180.

p. 46: "It was the . . . have ever seen." Ibid., p. 177.

p. 47: "Nothing looks . . . the roadbed." Ibid., p. 117.

CHAPTER 3: ATTACKING THE MOUNTAINS

p. 49: "We put a . . . repaired the break." Kraus, p. 163.

p. 52: "good engineers . . . the undertaking preposterous." Ambrose, p. 156.

p. 56: "They were a . . . rocks and earth." *Van Nostrand's Engineering Magazine,* 2–3,
    p. 436. CPRPHM.

p. 63: "The old engine . . . geography or geology." CPRPHM.

CHAPTER 4: A WILD EXCURSION

p. 66: "No one will . . . built the railroad." Ambrose, p. 213.

p. 66: "It was worth . . . the great work." Sabin, p. 175.

p. 67: "And tomorrow shall . . . in one day!" Ambrose, p. 283.

p. 69: "It was but . . . I ever saw." Barter, p. 40.

p. 70: "skinny expert riders . . . risk death daily." Savage, p. 25.

p. 72: "Wonderful indeed is . . . might and main." Brown, p. 81.

p. 74: "No railroad excursion . . . any other country." Ibid., p. 67.

p. 76: "Type of the . . . of the continent." Whitman, "To a Locomotive in Winter."

p. 77: "When I meet . . . to inhabit it." Thoreau, p. 153.

p. 82: "Whereas, An excursion . . . for this excursion." Mayer and Vose, p. 66.

p. 83: "the most important . . . in the world." Brown, p. 70.

p. 84: "It's hard to realize . . . short a time." UPRM.

p. 85: "There is nothing . . . is not wonderful." Ambrose, p. 174.

CHAPTER 5: TUNNELS, SNOW, AND NEVADA AT LAST

p. 88: "These storms made . . . twisting their tails." Kraus, p. 146.

p. 88: "The Chinese lived . . . under the snow." Williams, p. 143.

p. 90: "Perseverance alone [has] conquered." Ambrose, p. 324.

p. 91: "created one of . . . in American history." CPRPHM.

p. 91: "these storms were grand." Williams, p. 160.

p. 91: "Snow slides or . . . were dug out." Mayer and Vose, p. 43.

pp. 91–92: "There was constant . . . their frozen hands." CPRPHM.

p. 92: "Some of these . . . hundred feet long." Mayer and Vose, p. 53.

p. 93: "a stunner . . . like a comet." *Snowshoers of the Lost Sierra,* April 2013.

p. 94: "it was found . . . at great expense." Ambrose, p. 381.

p. 94: "It was decided . . . no alternative." Mayer and Vose, p. 49.

p. 96: "timbered . . . line-of-battle ships." Williams, p. 209.

p. 97: "They have conquered the snow." Ambrose, p. 304.

p. 97: "most consistent and debilitating enemy." CPRPHM.

p. 97: "The approaches to . . . [still] at work." Gillis, Speech before the American Society of Civil
Engineers, January 5, 1870. CPRPHM.

p. 99: "It was necessary . . . the entire route." CPRPHM.

p. 99: "We hauled locomotives . . . [tons of supplies]." Brown, p. 98.

p. 101: "[The Chinese worker] . . . commerce and civilization." Kraus, p. 198.

CHAPTER 6: HELL ON WHEELS

p. 103: "We are out . . . frozen, looks bad." UPRM.

p. 104: "I will pledge . . . of the ground." Ambrose, p. 339.

p. 105: "[I] never saw . . . Jack drove." Brown, p. 64.

p. 105: "is to be . . . round houses, etc." Mark Junge, *"Union Pacific Depot, 1972."* UPRM.

p. 107: "Our indian troubles . . . caused a panic." Dodge, p. 18.

p. 108: "were defending . . . lands, their homelands." "The Transcontinental Railroad," *American Experience.*

p. 108: "May 22 [1867] . . . go well armed." Ambrose, p. 209.

p. 109: "Our citizens swarmed . . . the far west." *Sundance Times,* February 25, 1960. UPRM.

p. 109: "Yesterday, at 5 . . . the bustling city." Ambrose, p. 369.

p. 109: "rushed wildly to . . . we honor you." Ibid.

pp. 110–111: "1st Extravagant dress . . . these beautiful plains." Mayer and Vose, p. 108.

p. 112: "Before nightfall, Cheyenne . . . in the rear." Ambrose, p. 369.

p. 112: "Cheyenne is now . . . rest of mankind." Ibid.

pp. 113–114: "Every gambler in . . . in great requisition." Ibid., p. 352.

p. 114: "At North Platte . . . at each other." "The Transcontinental Railroad," *American Experience.*

p. 114: "I . . . believe that . . . of their contents." Mayer and Vose, p. 102.

pp. 114–116: "This congregation of . . . murder a day." Bowles, p. 56.

p. 116: "Like its predecessors . . . intricate for me." Library of Congress, *Evolution of the Conservation Movement,* p. 57. UPRM.

p. 117–119: "The Bear River City . . . on the jail." *Crofutt's Trans-Continental Tourists' Guide,* 1872. UPRM.

p. 117: "with a sorry . . . turned him down." UPRM.

p. 119: "This place is . . . killed there already." Mayer and Vose, p. 5.

CHAPTER 7: TRACKS ACROSS THE DESERT

p. 121: "a purely arid . . . absolutely no timber." CPRPHM.

p. 122: "Long lines of . . . finishing the roadbed." *Pacific Monthly* 19, p. 209. CPRPHM.

p. 124: "As I was moving . . . city of Reno." Kraus, p. 194.

p. 125: "The biggest little . . . in the world." Reno Chamber of Commerce, 2014.

p. 126: "[The tracklaying site] . . . evening [stopping] place." Mayer and Vose, p. 124.

p. 126: "Taking out my . . . than 28 minutes." Wheeler, p. 107.

pp. 128–129: "Sherman is gained . . . the Pacific slope." Nichols, p. 137.

p. 131: "We cheerfully yield . . . our highest ambitions." Brown, p. 107.

p. 131: "May your descent be rapid." "The Transcontinental Railroad," *American Experience.*

p. 131: "a structure of interlaced toothpicks." Brown, p. 107.

p. 132: "I have never . . . in my life." Casement Papers.

CHAPTER 8: A RACE FOR GLORY

p. 138: "We never went . . . could be laid." CPRPHM.

p. 138: "But for the . . . hardly be begun." Mayer and Vose, p. 129.

pp. 140–141: "We surely live . . . to go through." Ibid., p. 133.

p. 141: "It was acknowledged . . . people of Utah." Ambrose, p. 287.

p. 142: "There's not a . . . six thousand miles." Ibid., p. 322.

p. 143: "We laid the . . . during the summer." Dodge, p. 117.

p. 143: "Keep right on . . . have your reward." Ambrose, p. 306.

p. 144: "An Act to . . . the Pacific Ocean" Pacific Railway Act of 1863, Stat. National Archives.

p. 144: "Even a few . . . marvelous scratching posts." Williams, p. 11.

p. 146: "rails shall meet . . . one continuous line." Ambrose, p. 340.

p. 148: "Work is being . . . wagons and men." Mayer and Vose, p. 123.

pp. 148–149: "They bragged of . . . was ever known." Ambrose, p. 564.

p. 152: "The scene is . . . teams hauling tools." Ibid., p. 350.

p. 152: "I never saw . . . built behind them." Ibid.

p. 154: "We backed down . . . no guess work." Fulton. CPRPHM.

p. 155: "H. H. Minkler was the foreman . . . nobody lost a minute." Mayer and Vose, p. 165.

CHAPTER 9: CELEBRATION

p. 157: "The last blow . . . their rock cutting." Mayer and Vose, p. 171.

p. 158: "Between six and . . . be entirely completed." Ibid., p. 171.

p. 159: "The two opposing . . . is going fast." Ibid., p. 184.

p. 162: "We stood with . . . was completed." Bain, p. 662.

p. 162: "From the first . . . nor surpassed since." Dodge, p. 54.

p. 164: "This spike weighs . . . mementos." Mayer and Vose, p. 193.

p. 164: "There was one . . . across the Continent.'" Rhodes, p. 194.

p. 168: "What a howl . . . missed it! Yee!" Mayer and Vose, p. 198.

p. 168: "Everybody slapped everybody . . . missed it too.'" Ibid.

p. 168: "To everybody, keep . . . of the hammer." Ibid., p. 197.

p. 168: "Almost ready . . . is being offered." Rhodes, p. 197.

p. 169: "We have got . . . to be presented." Mayer and Vose, p. 197.

p. 172: "The spirit of . . . were there unseen." Williams, pp. 267–268.

p. 173: "In common with . . . have happily surmounted." Mayer and Vose, p. 206.

p. 173: "We have just . . . put it through.'" Ibid., p. 205.

p. 173: "Tis Finished . . . coming and fast too." "The Transcontinental Railroad," *American Experience.*

pp. 173–174: "The changes now . . . of modern times." Sandler, p. 63.

p. 175: "A journey over . . . modern comforts." Ibid., p. 28.

p. 175: "Every man . . . make the trip." Brown, p. 136.

p. 175: "I felt particularly . . . never be broken." Ibid., p. 169.

p. 178: "The soil is . . . the Great Plains." Ambrose, p. 271.

p. 179: "When you look . . . more or better?'" Dodge, p. 49.

BIBLIOGRAPHY

Ambrose, Steven E. *Nothing Like It in the World: The Men Who Built the Transcontinental Railroad, 1863–1869*. New York: Simon and Schuster, 2000.

Bain, David Haward. *Empire Express: Building the First Transcontinental Railroad*. New York: Viking, 1999.

Barter, James. *A Worker on the Transcontinental Railroad*. San Diego: Lucent Books, 2003.

Beebe, Lucius, and Charles Clegg. *Hear the Train Blow: A Pictorial Epic of America in the Railroad Age*. New York: Grosset and Dunlap, 1952.

Blumberg, Rhonda. *Full Steam Ahead: The Race to Build a Transcontinental Railroad*. Washington, D.C.: National Geographic, 1996.

Bowles, Samuel. *Our New West: Records of Travel between the Mississippi River and the Pacific Ocean*. New York: Bibliographical Center for Research, 2009.

Brown, Dee. *Hear That Lonesome Whistle Blow: Railroads in the West*. New York: Holt, Rinehart and Winston, 1977.

Casement Papers, University of Wyoming.

Central Pacific Railroad Photographic History Museum.

Clark, Bill. "Snowshoers of the Lost Sierra," *Sierra Heritage,* April 2013.

Combs, Barry B. *Westward to Promontory: Building the Union Pacific across the plains and mountains*. Palo Alto, California: American West Publishing, 1969.

Dodge, Grenville M. *How We Built the Union Pacific Railway*. Washington: U.S. Government Printing Office, 1910.

Fulton, Robert. *Epic of the Overland*. New York: N. A. Kovach, 1954.

Gillis, J. G. Speech before the American Society of Civil Engineers.

Griswold, Wesley S. *A Work of Giants: Building the First Transcontinental Railroad*. New York: McGraw-Hill, 1962.

Hinckley, Helen. *Rails From the West: A Biography of Theodore D. Judah*. San Marino, California: Golden Spike Publications, 1969.

House Select Committee on the Pacific Railroad and Telegraph Report.

Jensen, Oliver. *The American Heritage History of Railroads in America*. New York: American Heritage, 1975.

Klein, Maury. *Union Pacific: The Birth of a Railroad*. New York: Doubleday, 1987.

Kraus, George. *High Road to Promontory: Building the Central Pacific across the High Sierra*. Palo Alto, California: American West, 1969.

Kung, S. W. *Chinese in American Life: Some Aspects of their History, Statues, Problems, and Contributions*. Seattle: University of Washington Press, 1962.

Lewis, Oscar. *The Big Four: The Story of Huntington, Stanford, Hopkins, and Crocker, and of the Building of the Central Pacific*. New York: Knopf, 1938.

Mayer, Lynne Rhodes, and Kenneth E. Vose. *Makin' Tracks: The Story of the Transcontinental Railroad in the Pictures and Words of the Men Who Were There*. New York: Praeger, 1975.

McCauge, James. *Moguls and Iron Men: The Story of the First Transcontinental Railroad*. New York: Harper, 1964.

Nichols, Joseph. *Condensed History of the Construction of the Union Pacific Railway.* Whitefish, Montana: Kessenger, 2010.

O'Connor, Richard. *Iron Wheels and Broken Men: The Railroad Barons and the Plunder of the West.* New York: Putnam, 1973.

Perkins, Jacob R. *Trails, Rails and War; The Life of General G. M. Dodge.* Indianapolis: Bobbs-Merrill, 1929.

Perry, Major Henry C. Unpublished manuscript.

Report on Railroads to the Senate of California.

Rothstein, Edward. "Looking at the Transcontinental Railroad as the Internet of 1869." *New York Times,* December 11, 1999.

Sabin, Edwin L. *Building the Pacific Railway.* Philadelphia: Lippincott, 1919.

Sandler, Martin W. *Inventors.* New York: HarperCollins, 2004.

Savage, Jeff. *Daring Pony Express Riders: True Tales of the Wild West.* Berkeley Heights, New Jersey: Enslow, 2012.

Steiner, Stan. *Fusang: The Chinese Who Built America.* New York: Harper, 1979.

Stover, John F. *Iron Road to the West: American Railroads in the 1850s.* New York: Columbia University Press, 1978.

Thoreau, Henry David. *Walden; Or, Life in the Woods.* New York: Dover, 1996.

Thorton, Willis. *The Nine Lives of Citizen Train.* New York: Greenberg, 1948.

"The Transcontinental Railroad." *American Experience.* Public Broadcasting Service.

Tung, Williams L. *The Chinese in America, 1820–1973: A Chronology and Fact Book*. Dobbs Ferry, New York: Oceana, 1974.

Union Pacific Railroad Museum.

Wheeler, Keith. *The Railroaders*. Alexandria, Virginia: Time-Life Books, 1973.

White, John H., Jr. *American Locomotives: An Engineering History, 1830–1880*. Baltimore: Johns Hopkins Press, 1968.

Whitman, Walt. *The Complete Poems*. New York: Penguin, 2005.

Williams, John Hoyt. *A Great and Shining Road: The Epic Story of the Transcontinental Railroad*. Lincoln: University of Nebraska Press, 1996.

Wilson, Neil C., and Frank J. Taylor. *Southern Pacific: The Roaring Story of a Fighting Railroad*. New York: McGraw-Hill, 1952.

PHOTOGRAPHY CREDITS

INDEX

Page numbers in italics indicate images.

ACKNOWLEDGMENTS

I am most grateful to Candlewick's Rachel Smith for the book's beautiful design. And I wish to thank Elizabeth Uhrig and Hannah Mahoney for the meticulous way in which every fact and quote was checked and authenticated. I am most appreciative of the help I received from Ginger Mayo, Ellen Sandberg, Virginia Allen, Abby Cape, and Andrew Gutterson. Finally, if this remarkable story has been brought to life in the way it deserves, it is due to Hilary Van Dusen. Thank you, Hilary, for sharing my enthusiasm, for shaping this volume, and for being my friend as well as noble editor.